WHAT THE
WORLD
IS COMING TO

A COMMENTARY ON THE BOOK OF

REVELATION

VERSE BY VERSE

Chuck Smith

THE WORD
FOR TODAY

P.O. Box 8000 • Costa Mesa, CA 92628 • 800-272-WORD (9673) • Web site: www.twft.com

WHAT THE WORLD IS COMING TO

© 2006 The Word For Today
P.O. Box 8000, Costa Mesa, CA 92628
(800) 272-WORD
www.twft.com
ISBN 10: 0–936728–48–5
ISBN 13: 978-0–936728–48–3
Second Printing 2009

Scriptural quotations are based on the King James Version of the Bible unless otherwise specified. Translational emendations, amplifications and paraphrases are by the author.

Library of Congress Cataloging in Publication Data:

Smith, Chuck
What the world is coming to.
Includes bibliographic references.
I. Bible. N.T. Revelation—Commentaries. I. Title.
BS2825.3.S57 228.06 77–3186

PRINTED IN THE UNITED STATES OF AMERICA

TABLE OF CONTENTS

Preface.. 1

Forewarning.. 3

CHAPTER 1
The Revelation.. 7

CHAPTER 2
Four Messages.. 25

CHAPTER 3
Three Messages 39

CHAPTER 4
The Rapture.. 45

CHAPTER 5
Who Owns the Earth?.................................... 53

CHAPTER 6
Bad News.. 61

CHAPTER 7
Two Special Groups....................................... 73

CHAPTER 8
Calamities 81

CHAPTER 9
Misery, Woe, and Suffering............................ 87

CHAPTER 10
Foreshadowing of the King............................. 99

CHAPTER 11
Two Special Agents 103

CHAPTER 12
People and Places 115

CHAPTER 13
The Antichrist.. 121

CHAPTER 14
Final Warning... 129

CHAPTER 15
The Plagues are Coming!................................ 137

CHAPTER 16
A World of Despair.. 141

CHAPTER 17
Counterfeit Church.. 153

CHAPTER 18
Bankruptcy.. 163

CHAPTER 19
Jesus Comes Again 173

CHAPTER 20
The Perfect Government................................... 179

CHAPTER 21
Our New Address... 197

CHAPTER 22
Peace Like a River 205

PREFACE

Many people say, "Stay out of the book of Revelation. That's a sealed book and you really can't understand it." It's true that, by attempting to interpret Revelation, people have done many weird things with it. But in reality it's a book that was not intended to be sealed. It was intended to be read and understood.

In this commentary on the book of Revelation we have sought to express concepts and conclusions drawn after years of study. We do not ask you to accept them just because we have stated them, but we urge you to search the Scriptures to see if these things be so.

The Bible says,

These [people of Berea] were more noble than those in Thessalonica, in that they received the word with all readiness of mind, and searched the Scriptures daily, whether those things were so (Acts 17:11).

The Scriptures tell us to "prove all things" and to "hold fast that which is good" (1 Thessalonians 5:21).

FOREWARNING

"THE END OF THE WORLD IS NEAR."

What statement used to be associated with old, gray bearded men walking barefooted in long robes with sandwich boards over their shoulders? The front of the board read "Repent" and the back read "The end of the world is near." We used to pass them off as crackpots and laugh at such a thought or idea.

But lately I've been reading not the wild fanatical statements of some old, so-called prophet but, rather, the statements of men of science, men with a Ph.D. who are highly respected for their knowledge. These men have studied the environmental conditions of the earth. Do you know what they're saying? They're saying, "The end of the world is near."

In fact, these experts are saying that man has anywhere from fourteen to forty years left upon this planet until we have so totally raped our natural resources that we can no longer survive. These men with their doctorates, who are carefully studying the balances of nature, are saying that the end of the world is near.

Is this possible? Can we really believe these ecologists? Are we really destroying nature's balances? Are we really wiping out hundreds of species, are we depleting our energy resources, and destroying the environment around us? Is it true that certain birds cannot hatch their eggs because of the DDT deposits in the eggshells? Is it true that the earth's ozone blanket is steadily disappearing? Are such things really happening? Maybe they're just trying to scare us.

However, they aren't the only ones warning us. Our militarists are telling us that the end of the world is near. They're warning us that if man engages in a full-scale nuclear war, we'll exterminate ourselves from the face of the earth and it will be the end of civilization.

In the face of these warnings, the United States continues to maintain its nuclear arsenal and the systems to deliver nuclear bombs upon our enemies. By the same token, our enemies are maintaining their nuclear arsenals and the means of delivering them upon the United States. The real danger is the widespread proliferation of nations now possessing nuclear weapons. We're in this mad war of building these huge nuclear arsenals. And already there are enough nuclear weapons stockpiled to obliterate mankind from the face of the earth.

Not only are the ecologists and militarists warning us, but so are the diplomats. Those analysts who study world conditions tell us that the world is sitting on a powder keg—and the fuse is being lit in the Middle East. At any time the situation can explode into a full-scale conflagration of the great world powers. The end of the world is near.

Is it possible that man could come to the end of an era? Don't we just go on forever, one society replacing another, one generation following another, on and on and on? Hasn't man cried this before? What do they mean, "The end of the world is near"?

The Answer—When Christians talk about the end of the world, they mean something different than the scientists. The scientists are talking about the end of mankind. Christians are talking about the end of the *cosmos*. This Greek word for *world* means "the set order." Christians are talking about the end of the present world order which is governed by Satan and in rebellion against God.

Man has had his day, and the day of man's attempt to govern himself is about to close. For a long time we've sought to govern ourselves and to live independently from God. We've tried about every conceivable form of government. We've sought for equality and justice. We've replaced one system of government with another. But we've proven, by the variety of governmental forms tried, that it's impossible for man to govern himself without falling into corruption. Even communism, the newest form, has already slipped into an irrevocable form of corruption from which there is no recovery.

What's the answer? What's the answer to the world's cries for peace, and the world's cries for love, and the world's cries for dwelling together in harmony? There is no answer except Jesus Christ.

We who are of the church look for a new form of government—a monarchy that embraces the entire world. We're waiting for our King to come and set up that monarchy. We're waiting for righteousness to cover the earth as the waters cover the seas. This glorious coming Kingdom and the momentous events surrounding its establishment are described to us in the prophetic book of Revelation.

CHAPTER 1

THE REVELATION

The Bible is unique and different from any other book in the world. It is a book that still stands today after years and years of criticism. It has been hammered on by all kinds of people for thousands of years. The hammers have worn out but the book still remains.

The Bible took over two thousand years to write and includes more than forty different authors. Yet, it is one, beautiful, continuous story of God's love and God's plan for sinning man.

The book of Revelation, written by the apostle John, is the last book of the Bible. It is divided into three sections or divisions. In Revelation 1:19 John was told by the angel to "write the things which you have seen, and the things which are, and the things which shall be after these things."

In chapter one, John wrote the things which he had seen—the vision of Jesus Christ. This is the first section of the book.

In chapters two and three, John wrote the things which are the letters of Jesus to the seven churches of Asia dealing with—things concerning the church, the ministry of the church, and the witness of the church in the world. These letters are the second section of the book and they describe the various periods of church history.

From Revelation 4 onward, the third section of Revelation, John prophesied those things which are to take place after the church has been taken out of the world—the future which is about to unfold before us.

REVELATION 1:1-2

The head of your King James Bible says "The Revelation of St. John the Divine." That is not accurate. That is man's heading. The book of Revelation does not reveal St. John the Divine. It reveals Jesus Christ.

We get the truth in verse one: "The Revelation of Jesus Christ." The word *revelation* is a translation of the Greek word *"apokalypsis"* which literally means "unveiling."

Picture, if you will, a draped statue that is about to be dedicated in front of city hall. The band is playing, the mayor gives a speech, and the artist who carved the statue tells about designing it. Then, the dramatic moment comes and the canvas is lifted. Everybody sees this statue that will now adorn city hall for the next century. That lifting-off of the canvas in the Greek is the word *apokalypsis.* It is taking off the wraps so you can see. The book of Revelation is the unveiling of Jesus Christ. So rather than being a sealed book, as some claim, it is taking the wraps off so that we might see Jesus in His future glory.

It is extremely important for you to know what God is and who Jesus Christ is. Some of you are totally ignorant concerning God. Your hearts are darkened. You have no knowledge of Him. Some of you have a veil over your eyes and heart, and you really don't *want* any knowledge of God. The Bible states, "The fool has said in his heart, There is no God" (Psalm 14:1). The man is a fool who doesn't seek to know God.

God has spoken to man. In times past He spoke by the prophets. In these last days he has spoken to us by His own dear Son "whom He has appointed heir of all things, by whom also He made the worlds" (Hebrews 1:2). Jesus Christ is the faithful witness of what God is. If you want to know what God is like, you can look to Jesus Christ and understand what God is all about.

> The Revelation [or unveiling] of Jesus Christ, which God gave unto Him, to show unto His servants things which must shortly come to pass; and He sent and signified it by His angel unto His servant John (Rev. 1:1).

Here we find the route by which this revelation came to us. God gave it to Jesus Christ, showing Him the glory that should be revealed. Concerning the cross the Bible said, "Who for the joy that was set before Him endured the cross, despising the shame" (Hebrews 12:2). This book of Revelation, to a great extent, is the joy that was set before Jesus Christ as the Father showed Him the place that He would have in the ages to come.

Jesus, in turn, gave the revelation to His angel who brought it to His servant, John, "who bore record of the word of God, and of the testimony of Jesus Christ, and of all things that he saw" (Rev. 1:2).

In his first epistle John wrote,

That which we have seen with our eyes, which we have looked upon, and our hands have handled, of the Word of life... That which we have seen and heard declare we unto you, that you also may have fellowship with us: and truly our fellowship is with the Father, and with His Son Jesus Christ (1 John 1:1, 3).

John is the faithful recorder writing the things that he saw and heard, writing as the Lord dictated to him. This revelation came by vision as well as by voice. The people in the vision, the spiritual entities that John saw, were conversing with him and explaining many of the things that he saw.

REVELATION 1:3

Included in this book of Revelation is a built-in blessing.

Blessed is he that reads, and they that hear the words of this prophecy, and keep those things which are written therein: for the time is at hand (Rev. 1:3).

The blessing is upon those that *hear* and those that *read* this book. It was addressed to the seven churches in Asia. It was actually intended to be read in the churches and, no doubt, a copy was made for each church.

In those days they did not have bookstores or racks in the supermarkets. Writing material was very scarce. The early writing material was papyrus from Egypt. Then Egypt put a premium on it and began a papyrus embargo in order to raise prices and put the squeeze on the world. So, in Pergamos, they invented parchment as a writing material. But it, too, was very scarce. At the time of Christ there were great libraries but very few people had any books of their own. They did, however, have the materials to write personal letters. Each of the churches received a copy of the letter and it was to be read aloud in the church.

Much of the church service in those days was given to the reading of the various epistles and this book of Revelation. The blessings are to those that hear, to those that read the words of this prophecy, and to those that *keep* the things that are written in it.

Notice that John himself calls it a prophecy. Thus, when we read it we must look to the future. It's speaking of things that shall happen.

Interpretations—There are various interpretations of the book of Revelation. There's the *preterist* interpretation of the book of Revelation, which seeks to make all the events correspond to the church's struggle against imperial Rome. It sees the whole book transpiring during the period of Roman history when the church went through great persecution by various emperors. It interprets the book as completed and fulfilled.

There is the *historic* interpretation which sees the book of Revelation as the history of the church's struggle against the world systems. This goes beyond the Roman period and follows through to the present time.

There is also the *spiritual* interpretation which confuses things so completely that nobody understands what is what. This interpretation spiritualizes everything so nothing means what it says. Everything is interpreted as a spiritual allegory. When you spiritualize the Scriptures you remove any authority or teaching from them, because every man is free to interpret the spiritual allegory as he desires.

Then there is the *futurist* interpretation of the book of Revelation. I personally feel that the futurist view is the correct view. With the futurist view you can read the book and believe that it meant what it said, and it said what it meant. You don't have to start twisting things to make them fit here and there, and changing them to fit some scheme. The futurist view takes the revelation just as it says, to be understood just as it is.

REVELATION 1:4-5

> John to the seven churches which are in Asia: Grace be unto you, and peace, from Him who is, and who was, and who is to come; and from the seven Spirits who are before His throne (Rev. 1:4).

The number seven is mentioned over and over throughout this prophecy. Seven is sometimes called God's perfect number because it represents completeness or totality. Seven days make a complete week, seven notes comprise the musical scale, and seven colors are in the rainbow. Thus, seven churches would indicate the complete church.

Geographically, these churches complete a small circle. There were many more churches in Asia Minor than these seven; one of the major churches, Colosse, was not addressed here. But, because seven is the number of completeness, these seven present us with the complete history of the church.

In this prophecy we also have the seven seals, the seven trumpet judgments, the seven thunders, and the seven vials of God's wrath—all of which demonstrate God's complete judgment on the earth.

It is also worth noticing that the number eight is the number of new beginnings. The eighth day starts the new week; after seven musical notes the eighth note starts the new upper scale. Since each letter of the Greek alphabet carries a numeric equivalent, it is interesting that the total numeric value of the names for Jesus in the Greek are all divisible by eight—Jesus, *Christos, Kurios*. He is the new beginning, and we have a new beginning in Christ.

"Grace be unto you, and peace, from Him who is, and who was, and who is to come." This is God's eternal character. God is past, He is present, and He is future. He was, He is, and He is to come. He's all these at the same time. Everything is the "eternal now" with God.

"And from the seven Spirits which are before His throne." Here (and in Revelation 3, 4 and 5) we read of the seven Spirits before the throne of God. Again, the number seven indicates the completeness of the work of the Holy Spirit. The prophet Isaiah, speaking of the ministry of Jesus Christ declared,

> The **Spirit of the LORD** shall rest upon Him, the Spirit of **wisdom** and **understanding**, the Spirit of **counsel** and **might**, the Spirit of **knowledge** and of the **fear of the LORD** (Isaiah 11:2).

Thus, the seven-fold working of the Holy Spirit is defined and described.

John sends the blessings from God, from the Holy Spirit, "and from Jesus Christ, who is the faithful witness" (Rev. 1:5). Jesus Christ is the faithful witness of what God is. He came to reveal the Father.

The night in which He was betrayed, Jesus was talking with His disciples. Philip cried to Him, "Lord, show us the Father, and it will suffice us." Jesus said, "Have I been so long a time with you, and yet you have not known me, Philip? He that has seen me has seen the Father; then why do you say, Show us the Father?" (John 14:8–9).

Today, God wants to reveal Himself through you. It is God's purpose that the world sees Him through you. That is a very heavy obligation on our part. Jesus said, "You shall be witnesses unto me" (Acts 1:8). Our lives are to bear witness of Jesus Christ and who He is.

The word *witness* in Greek is "*martus*," from which we get our English word "martyr." "Jesus Christ, who is the faithful witness [martyr], and the first begotten of the dead" (Rev. 1:5).

This phrase *first begotten* doesn't mean the first in time but the first in *priority*. *First begotten* is speaking of prominence. It refers to Jesus Christ as the most important one ever raised from the dead.

Also, Jesus was begotten of the dead unto eternal life never to die again. Others had been raised from the dead only to die a second time. But Jesus arose never to die again. In this sense, He is "the first begotten of the dead."

He is "the prince [ruler] of the kings of the earth" (Rev. 1:5). This is the title and position that Jesus will have during the kingdom age. God "has made him a little lower than the angels, and has crowned him with glory and honor" (Psalm 8:5). We see a world that is in chaos and under the power and dominion of Satan. But we're looking for that glorious coming kingdom when Jesus will assume His position as the ruler of the kings of the earth.

Revelation 1:5 describes Jesus and His relationship to you: "Unto Him that loved us." Never doubt the love of Jesus Christ for you! Satan will seek to have you doubt that love. He'll whisper, "You've been bad! God certainly doesn't love you now. You've failed! You haven't lived up to His standards. Jesus doesn't love bad little boys." That isn't true. Jesus loves you no matter what your condition. "While we were yet sinners, Christ died for us" (Romans 5:8). Jesus died for the ungodly. And if, while you were a sinner and rebelling against Him, He loved you enough to die for you; how much more shall you experience the fullness of that love and grace now that you've opened your heart to Him and sought to walk after Him?

Unto Him that loved us, and [because He loved us] washed us from our sins in His own blood (Rev. 1:5).

For the blood of Jesus Christ, God's son, cleanses a man from all sin. In His love, Jesus shed His blood and washed you from all of your sins. For "all we like sheep have gone astray; we have turned every one to his own way; and the LORD has laid on Him the iniquity of us all" (Isaiah 53:6). He died in our place.

REVELATION 1:6-7

"And has made us kings and priests unto God" (Rev. 1:6). Or, more literally, "has made us a kingdom of priests unto God."

A priest of the Old Testament had a two-fold ministry. First of all, he represented the people before God. While doing this, he wore a breastplate with twelve stones representing the twelve tribes of Israel. His second function was to represent God to the people. He was the go-between for the people and God. Jesus is our Great High Priest who has come down to the earth and represented God to us and has now entered into heaven for us. There He is representing us before the Father (Hebrews 4:14).

In the kingdom age we will be a kingdom of priests, going before Christ *for* the people and representing Christ *to* the people. "To Him be glory and dominion for ever and ever. Amen" (Rev. 1:6).

Jesus Christ will be coming back to the earth very soon to establish the Kingdom of God. The age of man is almost over. The world is being destroyed by man.

And except those days should be shortened, there should no flesh be saved: but for the elect's sake those days shall be shortened (Matthew 24:22).

We're living in those days that are now being shortened. God is doing a quick work in these days. We're coming to the end of the age and Jesus will soon be returning.

When He returns we'll be returning with Him. "Behold, the Lord comes with ten thousands of His saints" (Jude 14). "When Christ, who is our life, shall appear, then shall you also appear with Him in glory" (Colossians 3:4). He will be coming in clouds with great glory to establish the kingdom of God, and we will be reigning with Him for one thousand years upon the earth. The Bible speaks of a yearly convocation when we shall gather in Jerusalem to bring the offerings and the glories of the nations unto Him (Zechariah 14:16). The Scripture doesn't specify the nature of our reign or what it will be like, but it's going to be great!

"Behold, He comes with clouds" (Rev. 1:7). There are many places where the coming of Jesus Christ is mentioned as coming in clouds. "And they shall see the Son of man coming in the clouds of heaven with power and great glory" (Matthew 24:30). Daniel prophesied, "One like the Son of man came with the clouds of heaven, and came to the Ancient of Days" (Daniel 7:13).

When Jesus was with His disciples on the Mount of Olives, He ascended into heaven and a cloud received Him. The angels (the two men in white apparel) said,

> Men of Galilee, why stand gazing up into heaven? This same Jesus, which is taken up from you into heaven, shall so come in like manner as you saw Him go into heaven (Acts 1:1).

"Behold, He comes with clouds." This could be the clouds of saints, the great cloud of witnesses, with which Jesus shall return. "And every eye shall see Him" (Rev. 1:7).

When God comes again, it's not going to be a secret coming. It won't be in some secret chamber and revealed only to a specified, elect few. The whole world is going to know when He returns.

"And every eye shall see Him." This surely refutes the theory that the coming of Jesus Christ was a secret event in 1848, 1878, 1917, 1918, or one of the many dates that people have given for His coming. When you confront them, quoting "Every eye shall see Him," they say that Jesus came in a secret chamber, and only the real initiated knew that He came. But Jesus said, "If they shall say unto you... Behold, He is in the secret chambers; believe it not" (Matthew 24:26). "Every eye shall see Him, and they also which pierced Him," that is, the Jewish people (Rev. 1:7).

Zechariah also prophesied this coming again of Jesus Christ. He said the Jews will say unto Him, "What are these wounds in Your hands?" (Zechariah 13:6). Zechariah said, "And they shall look upon Me whom they have pierced, and they shall mourn for Him" (Zechariah 12:10).

The Jews will weep over the fact that they failed to recognize Jesus as the Messiah. They will actually bewail and mourn the spiritual blindness that had gripped their nation in the time of Christ and is gripping their nation even now.

"They also which pierced Him: and all people of the earth shall wail because of Him" (Rev. 1:7). Zechariah describes the bewailing as a woman travailing for her only son who had died (Zechariah 12:10). The Jews will weep and cry over their national blindness.

REVELATION 1:8-9

"I am Alpha and Omega, the beginning and the ending, says the Lord, which is, and which was, and which is to come, the Almighty" (Rev. 1:8).

In describing His eternal nature, God declares that He is the Alpha and Omega. That is the Greek for A and Z—the first and the last letters of the Greek alphabet. God is the totality. He is the beginning and the ending. It all started with God and it all ends with God. He is, He was, He is to come. He is eternal.

In Revelation 21:6 Jesus says the same thing. From this we conclude that Jesus also is eternal—co-eternal with the Father, the Alpha and Omega, the beginning and the ending.

John describes the circumstances by which the vision first came to him. "I, John, who also am your brother, and companion in tribulation" (Rev. 1:9). The beautiful humility of John. He is not coming on as a great leader demanding submission to his authority. He calls himself a brother.

God never intended a spiritual hierarchy to be established within the church. We're all part of one body. That is so glorious! God has no favorites or specials. "God is no respecter of persons" (Acts 10:34), which means that God is as interested in you as He is in Billy Graham and as He was in Dwight Moody, Charles Finney, John Wesley, John Knox or Martin Luther. God didn't love them any more than He loves you. God didn't listen to them any more readily than He will listen to you.

John said, "I'm a brother and a companion." Pray to God that men within the ministry today will have the same attitude as a brother and a companion. As Paul said, "We are laborers together with God" (1 Corinthians 3:9). We're all one in this body of Christ. We all share together. We're all just people. When the crowd was going to worship Paul, he tore his clothes and said "Hey, I'm just a man like the rest of you! I'm no god!" (Acts 14:14–15).

We're all equal in the eyes of the Lord. God considers us as individuals and loves us as individuals. He is no respecter of persons. You can't buy God. You can't influence God. You can't con God. He is the same to everybody. You can't bully or pressure Him. Looking at Him, what can you do for Him? People are always trying to peddle influence in the world. You can't peddle any influence with God. He treats us all alike and loves us all the same.

"John, who also am your brother, and companion in tribulation, and in the kingdom and patience of Jesus Christ" (Rev. 1:9). The patience of Jesus Christ is the waiting for Jesus Christ to return.

James wrote, "Be patient therefore, brethren, unto the coming of the Lord. Behold, the farmer waits for the precious [perfect] fruit of the earth" (James 5:7). Peter encouraged us to have patience in waiting for the Lord (2 Peter 3:8–15). Paul also encouraged us to have patience—waiting for the coming of the Lord (1 Thessalonians 1:10).

John "was in the isle that is called Patmos, for the Word of God, and for the testimony of Jesus Christ" (Rev. 1:9).

Persecutions—The first major persecution under the Roman empire took place as the result of Nero's reign. Thousands of Christians were crucified and executed. During Nero's persecution Paul and Peter were both killed.

Then under the reign of Domitian (AD 81–96) the second persecution took place. About forty thousand more Christians were put to death for their faith. It was during this time that John was exiled to the island of Patmos. There, John received these visions from the Lord.

John, the overseer of the church in Ephesus, was exiled to the Island of Patmos because of the Word of God and his testimony of Jesus Christ. According to Eusebius, the church historian, John was boiled in oil. This, though, had no adverse effect on him, and he was sent to the small, craggy, rocky island of Patmos off the coast of Asia Minor, about thirty-two miles from Ephesus in the Aegean Sea.

John was exiled to the Island of Patmos because God had a special message to give him. God had to get him in a quiet place, away from the disturbances and pressures of the church in Ephesus. Whether or not he was still on the island of Patmos when he actually wrote the letter is uncertain. After his exile on Patmos (c.96 AD), John returned to Ephesus where he eventually died. It is possible that when he came back to Ephesus, John wrote this book of Revelation, the last of the New Testament canon of Scriptures.

REVELATION 1:10A

"I was in the Spirit on the Lord's day" (Rev. 1:10a). This can have two possible meanings. First, it can mean that the revelation came to John on a Sunday. It seems that early in the church, Sunday was referred to as the Lord's day, being the eighth day and the first day of the week. Sunday was the day in which Jesus rose from the dead. It was a day when the church was accustomed to gathering together. Paul told the Corinthians to bring their offerings when they gathered together on the first day of the week so there would be no collections when he came (1 Corinthians 16:1–2). In Acts the Christians gathered together on the first day of the week to break bread (Acts 20:7).

Early in church history Sunday was called the Lord's day. It was not a change that was brought about by Constantine, which the Seventh-day Adventists would have you believe. In fact, Tertullian, who wrote almost two centuries before Constantine, said that Sunday should be the only day on which the church would have communion, because Jesus rose on the first day of the week. Of course that was his logic and not necessarily true, but it shows that the first day of the week was set apart early in church history as a time for the worship of Christ. John may have been saying that he was in the Spirit or in a spiritual trance on Sunday.

A Time Chamber—With equal authority from the Greek, Revelation 1:10a could be translated, "I was in the Spirit unto the day of the Lord" rather than "on the Lord's day." This would mean that the Lord put John into a time chamber, so to speak, and transferred him to the end of the age. There John saw all the battles and judgments that are described in the Revelation. The Lord took him out in time to the day of the Lord, and John recorded these events as though he were actually there.

When Jesus took His disciples to the Mount of Trans-figuration, He took them into a kind of time chamber. Prior to this, He had said, "Some of you here are not going to taste of death, until you see the Son of man coming in his kingdom." Six days later He took Peter, James and John up to the top of the high mountain. There He was transfigured before them. His raiment was white as the light and His face did shine like the sun. There appeared unto them Moses and Elijah talking to Jesus about things of the kingdom (Matthew 16:28–17:4).

What happened? The disciples were taken to a time zone which is yet future to us. They saw the Lord's future glory. He was talking with Moses and Elijah about the kingdom age.

John, possibly, was also taken in a time chamber by the Lord. It would be very easy for God, who is eternal, to put John into that eternal dimension for a moment and take him out to the end of the age where he could see all these things that are going to happen.

God has already seen the things that are transpiring on the earth today. He has omniscience. He knows all things. God knows exactly what the next move will be, how it'll take place, where it's going to transpire. Your life is like a rerun as far as God is concerned.

And so, it was very likely that John saw the future coming of Jesus Christ. I personally believe that this is the intent here. "I was taken in the Spirit unto the day of the Lord."

REVELATION 1:10B-16

John continues the vision: I "heard behind me a great voice, as of a trumpet, saying, I am Alpha and Omega, the first and the last: and, What you see, write in a book, and send it unto the seven churches which are in Asia; unto Ephesus, and unto Smyrna, and unto Pergamos, and unto Thyatira, and unto Sardis, and unto Philadelphia, and unto Laodicea. And I turned to see the voice that spoke with me. And being turned, I saw seven golden candlesticks" (Rev. 1:10b–12).

The "seven golden candlesticks" takes us back to the tabernacle in the wilderness (Exodus 25:31–39). A part of its furnishings was a golden *menorah*, a candelabrum with three branches protruding from each side of the main stem. These seven sticks had little cups that served as candleholders. This furnished the light in the sanctuary.

These seven golden candlesticks represented what the nation Israel was to be to the world. It was to be God's light to the world.

The seven golden candlesticks, when applied to the church, show God's intention for the church in the world. The church is to be God's light in the world. Jesus said, "You are the light of the world" (Matthew 5:14).

And in the midst of the seven candlesticks One like unto the Son of Man, clothed with a garment down to the foot, and girded about the chest with a golden band (Rev. 1:13).

Jesus is walking in the midst of the seven golden candlesticks and is described as the Son of man. Jesus made reference to Himself as the Son of Man as well as the Son of God. The Son of Man was a prophetic reference to Daniel's prophecy concerning the second coming of Jesus Christ the King, and was one of the titles of the Messiah (Daniel 7:13–14).

John then describes a little bit of His clothing:

Clothed with a garment down to the foot, and girded about the chest with a golden band. His head and His hairs were white like wool, as white as snow; and His eyes were as a flame of fire; and His feet like fine brass, as if they burned in a furnace; and His voice as the sound of many waters. And He had in His right hand seven stars: and out of His mouth went a sharp two-edged sword: and His countenance was as the sun shining in His strength (Rev. 1:13–16).

His face was just brilliant, like looking into the sun, and He was walking in the midst of the candlesticks.

Jesus said, "Where two or three are gathered together in My name, there am I in the midst" (Matthew 18:20). Here John sees Jesus in the midst of His churches. Jesus is in the midst of His church as we gather together in His name. He is present with us. He has promised to bestow upon us His love, His grace, His kindness, His mercy, His Word. Jesus is here to minister to you and to your needs. He is still in the midst of the seven golden candlesticks—His church through the ages.

John saw Him holding the seven stars in His right hand. The seven stars are the seven angels of these churches (Rev. 1:20). The word *angel* translated in Greek means "messenger," which is usually the pastor. What joy and comfort to the pastor to realize that Jesus holds him.

This is the only description of Jesus Christ in the New Testament. We have one description of Him in the Old Testament in Daniel (Daniel 7:9–10). Revelation 1:13–16 is not a description of a suffering Savior but of our exalted Lord in His glory in heaven. John sees Him in His glory and describes Him in that glory.

Jesus said in His prayer in John 17, "Father, to those that You have given Me, that they might see Me in My glory that I had with You before the world was" (John 17:5, 24). He asked for that glory to be returned, and then He asked that we might see Him in that glory.

Here John sees Jesus and what He'll look like when we see
Him. His face is shining like the sun at noontime. His head and
His hair are like wool, white as snow. His eyes are like flames of
fire and His feet like fine brass heated to the point of
incandescence. His words sound like a great waterfall. Out of His
mouth is a sharp two-edged sword. "For the word of God is quick,
and powerful, and sharper than any two-edged sword" (Hebrews
4:12).

REVELATION 1:17-18

When John saw Him, he said, "I fell at His feet as dead. And
He laid His right hand upon me, saying to me, Fear not; I am the
first and the last" (Rev. 1:17).

John is really overwhelmed by the whole vision. Daniel, who
also received some pretty venerable visions, was always falling on
his face. He said, "And I, Daniel, fainted, and was sick certain
days... I was astonished at the vision" (Daniel 8:27). He was
actually sick as a result of some of these experiences of passing
through spiritual dimensions and receiving these spiritual
revelations. Paul the apostle received so much spiritual revelation
that it actually resulted in a thorn in his flesh (2 Corinthians 12:7).

Here is John falling on his face. On various occasions
throughout the book, John is falling down on his face. It would no
doubt be a very powerful sensation to go through these kinds of
experiences.

Jesus then laid His right hand on him and said,

Fear not; I am the first and the last: I am He that lives, and
was dead; and, behold, I am alive for evermore, Amen; and
have the keys of hell and of death (Rev. 1:17–18).

Jesus triumphed over hell. He triumphed over death. He rose
triumphant. He said, "I have the keys of hell and death," by which
He was speaking of releasing the prisoners. In Luke's gospel, Jesus
described hell as being in two compartments divided by a gulf. On
one side they were being comforted, the other side was tormented.

Isaiah prophesied concerning Jesus Christ:

The Spirit of the Lord GOD is upon Me; because the LORD has anointed Me to preach good tidings unto the meek... to proclaim liberty to the captives, and the opening of the prison to them that are bound" (Isaiah 61:1).

Referring to those that had died, those that were captive in hell, in the grave, Jesus said, "I have the keys of hell and of death." He opened up Hades and released those souls that were in prison.

Paul said that He who has ascended is the same one who first descended into the lower parts of the earth. When He ascended He led the captives from their captivity (Ephesians 4:8–9). Peter said that Jesus went and preached to those souls that were in prison (1 Peter 3:19). Jesus opened up hell and delivered Abraham and the others who by faith were believing and waiting for the coming Messiah.

REVELATION 1:19-20

The Key To The Book—The key to the book of Revelation is found here. The Lord said unto John, "Write the things which you have seen, and the things which are, and the things which shall be hereafter" (Rev. 1:19). The word *hereafter* in the Greek is *"meta tauta"* which means "after these things."

This command actually divides the book of Revelation into three sections. (1) The things that John saw, the vision of Christ in Revelation chapter one. (2) The things which are, which deals with the messages to the seven churches in Asia found in Revelation chapters two and three. (3) The things which shall be *meta tauta,* "after these things," chapters four through twenty-two. John sees the events of the future, the things that transpire after the church has finished its mission on the earth and has been removed.

It is significant that the fourth chapter of Revelation begins with this same phrase, *meta tauta,* "after these things." After *what* things? After the things of the church are completed. "I saw a door open in heaven: and the first voice which I heard was as of a

trumpet saying unto me, Come up here, and I will show you things
which must be after these things *[meta tauta]*" (Rev. 4:1).

Beginning with Revelation 4:1, we are dealing with things that
are future—things which have not yet taken place but shall take
place after the church's testimony is finished upon the earth. If you
follow this key, you'll find the divisions in the book of Revelation
easy to understand. (1) The things that John saw. (2) The things
which are. (3) The things which will be after these things.

Jesus explains to John the vision that he has seen. "The mystery
of the seven stars which you saw in my right hand, and the seven
golden candlesticks. The seven stars are the angels of the seven
churches" (Rev. 1:20).

The word *angels* actually means "messengers." They generally
refer to divine messengers, supernatural beings created by God. But
the word literally is "messenger." The "seven stars" are the
messengers of the seven churches. They could refer to the ministers
of those particular churches.

"And the seven candlesticks which you saw are the seven
churches" (Rev. 1:20). The "seven churches" symbolically speak of
completeness. I believe that in these messages we have a picture of
the complete church history.

There is a three-fold application of these messages. First, they
were written to the seven churches and dealt with problems within
the church at that very time (local application). Second, I believe
that there is an historic application in these messages, giving us the
seven periods of church history. Third, I believe that even today
this message is applicable because you can find these same
conditions in different churches today.

In many places these messages will apply directly to us.

CHAPTER 2
FOUR MESSAGES

REVELATION 2:1-3

E phesus—

"Unto the angel of the church of Ephesus write;
These things says He that holds the seven stars in
His right hand, who walks in the midst of the seven
golden candlesticks" (Rev. 2:1).

There are certain similarities in all the messages to the seven
churches. Each message begins with a description of Christ given
by Himself and then includes a description of Christ taken from
the vision in Revelation 1.

"From Him who is holding the seven stars and walking in the
midst of the seven golden candlesticks": a message from Jesus as He
walks in the midst of His church, holding the angels of the
churches.

To each of the churches Jesus declares His knowledge
concerning them. "I know your works" (Rev. 2:2).

Many times we think that we're hiding things from God. No
way! He knows our works. More than that, He knows the
motivation behind our works. Some of the works will be
burned—those done for vainglory (to be seen by men), about
which Jesus said, "You have your reward" (Matthew 6:2, 5). Every
man, one day, will be judged according to his works—what
manner or sort they are (Rev. 2:23, 20:13).

Jesus continues to the church of Ephesus, "I know your works,
and your labor, and your patience, and how you cannot bear them

which are evil: you have tried them which say they are apostles, and are not, and have found them liars" (Rev. 2:2).

In the early church there were itinerant ministers who went from church to church. There were two companies: those who were apostles (they claimed apostleship and the authority of apostleship), and those who went around as prophets ministering to the local bodies.

In time these traveling ministers became a problem in the church because of false prophets. These deceivers would come into a church and really rip things up. To guard against this, a manual was written to warn the church against the false prophets and how to spot them. If one came along and prophesied, "Thus says the Lord, 'Prepare a big turkey dinner!'"—he was not to eat of it. If he ate of it, he was a false prophet. If he declared to you by the Spirit that you were to give him gifts, he was a false prophet. He was to stay for two days. If he stayed any longer and tried to sponge off you, he was a false prophet. This advice was intended to keep these itinerants on the move and to prevent them from profiting from the churches.

In Ephesus the Christians exercised discernment on those who came in and claimed to be apostles but were not. "You found them to be liars." The Lord commended them for their discernment.

He commended them for their holiness. They would not bear those who were evil. He commended them for their work, their labor, and their patience. "And you have had patience for my name's sake, and has labored, and not fainted" (Rev. 2:3).

Ephesus was a working church according to Christ's description. In labor they did not faint. They had patience and discernment. They had all of these things going for them.

REVELATION 2:4-5

Return to Your First Love—Yet, the Lord said, "Nevertheless I have this against you, because you have left your first love" (Rev. 2:4).

Ephesus was a church that was still going through the motions but they had left the emotions. They were no longer motivated by the love of Jesus Christ. They were now being motivated by pressure, habit, form, or ritual.

What a sad day when your ministry turns into a job! Paul said, "For the love of Christ constrains us" (2 Corinthians 5:14). It was the love that drove Paul onward.

Though I speak with the tongues of men and of angels, and have not love, I am become as sounding brass, or a tinkling cymbal... And though I bestow all my goods to feed the poor... and I have not love, it profits me nothing (1 Corinthians 13:1–3).

I can have a lot of things going for me. I can be the hardest and most diligent worker in a church. I can give myself tirelessly to the spreading of the Gospel. But if I have not love, if I have left my first love, it profits me nothing. Jesus said that, though you have all this going for you, you have left your first love.

"Remember therefore from where you have fallen, and repent, and do the first works" (Rev. 2:5).

Many people say, "Oh, you've lost your first love." You don't lose it—you *leave* it. If you lose something, you never know where to pick it up again. You don't know where to find it. If you leave something, you know where to pick it up again. Jesus tells us how to return to our first love.

The three R's: "**Remember** therefore from where you have fallen." Remember that love that you once had? "**Repent.**" Then **Repeat.** "Do the first works." Come back to that first work of love. It is first above everything else. Do your first works over again, those works motivated and prompted by *love*.

To most of the churches Jesus said, "Repent." There is the necessity of repentance in most churches. There were only two to whom He didn't have to say "Repent."

Repent, and do the first works; or else I will come unto you quickly, and will remove your candlestick out of its place, except you repent (Rev. 2:5).

Unless there was a repentance, a return to that first love, Jesus would remove the candlestick from its place. Where was its place? In the presence of Christ, for He walked in the midst of the candlesticks. Jesus is saying, "I will not stay around a loveless church." This is a very solemn consideration.

Unfortunately, as we look at the church today—so filled with factions, fighting, and divisions—in many cases the candlestick has been removed from its place. You go to church but you don't feel the presence and the power of Jesus Christ. Instead, you feel the factions and all the pressures and strain. Jesus said, "I won't stay around a loveless church."

REVELATION 2:6-7

"But this you have: that you hate the deeds of the Nicolaitanes, which I also hate" (Rev. 2:6).

"Nicolaitanes" comes from two Greek words: *nikao* and *laos* meaning "establishing a priesthood over a laity." The church of Ephesus hated that establishment of a spiritual hierarchy. Jesus said, "Which I also hate."

Why? Because, in our minds, it suddenly puts some men closer to God than others. God doesn't want anyone to feel far from Him. He wants every man to feel close to Him. God doesn't want you to feel that you have to go through someone to get to Him. He wants you to come directly to Him in His Son Jesus Christ. Jesus has opened the door to God for every man alike, and He doesn't want anyone to stand in your way of coming to Him. To each church Jesus said, "He that has an ear, let him hear what the Spirit says unto the churches; To him that overcomes will I give..."

To each church there is a blessing to the overcomers. It is interesting to note, and I do bear witness, that in every church, even the most apostate, there are the individual overcomers who truly know Jesus Christ.

To the church of Ephesus He promised, "To him that overcomes will I give to eat of the tree of life, which is in the midst of the paradise of God" (Rev. 2:7).

In the Garden of Eden God had given to man the fruit of the trees for his meat. Two specific trees were mentioned. There was the tree of knowledge of good and evil which man was forbidden to eat, and the tree of life, which, if a man ate of it, he would live forever.

Adam and Eve had their choice of the trees. It would seem to me that they would have chosen immediately to eat of the tree of life. Why would they choose the tree of knowledge of good and evil over the tree of life? Why would they eat of its fruit before the fruit of the tree of life? The knowledge of good and evil, however, was more important to them than life.

In reality, man has the same choice today. You can't blame Adam for all your evils or troubles or ills, because God has given you the choice of the tree of life, if you'll just partake of it. The cross of Jesus Christ is life to those who believe and trust in Him. You have the opportunity to partake of that life in Christ.

A lot of people have intellectual hang-ups. They have made their intellect their god. Because they cannot fully understand or comprehend the meaning of the incarnation and its purpose—the substitutionary death of Christ—they do not partake of the tree of life, though the opportunity is there for them.

When Adam ate of the tree of knowledge of good and evil, God banished him from the Garden. The cherubim stood at the entrance to the Garden with a flaming sword to protect it lest man would return, eat of the tree of life, and live forever in his sins (Genesis 2:9, 16, 17; Genesis 3:24).

That cherubim was not stationed there as a judgment from God but as a representative of the mercy of God. God in His mercy didn't want man to go on forever in this corrupt, sinful body. For man's sake, He put the cherubim there to keep foolish man from the garden lest he would eat of the tree of life and go on living forever in a body corrupted by sin.

Too many times people see God as a God of judgment and wrath when, in reality, He's a God of love and mercy. But they misinterpret the mercy of God for judgment. God was protecting man from himself by placing the cherubim at the entrance to the Garden to keep man from reentering.

The tree of life is in the midst of the paradise of God, wherever that may be. He that overcomes will have the opportunity to eat of that tree. We'll partake of the tree of life!

Historically Ephesus is the early church, the apostolic church, that existed up until the time of the death of John (c.99 AD). Even at the time of John's writing, the fire of love had begun to wane a bit in the early church. When they first started out they were fervent. They went everywhere preaching the Gospel. The love of Christ was driving them throughout the world. Now, they were already becoming a bit established, leaving their first love.

REVELATION 2:8-9

Smyrna—Historically, Smyrna is the church that followed Ephesus. It continued for the next couple of centuries (second to fourth centuries) and went through such tremendous persecution from the Roman government. It is thought that perhaps as many as six million Christians were martyred for their faith during the Roman government's attempt to wipe out Christianity.

"Unto the angel of the church in Smyrna" (Rev. 2:8).

If the "angel" refers to the local bishop of the church, the bishop of Smyrna was Polycarp, a disciple of John, martyred in his 90's. The government planned to kill this aged man by burning him at the stake. As the wood was gathered around him, the executioner said, "I hate to see an old man die. Just recant Christ and we'll set you free. Then you can live your last days in peace."

Polycarp said, "For over eighty years I have served my Lord and Savior, Jesus Christ. Not once has He denied me. I shall not deny Him."

The executioner said, "The fire will be hot."

Polycarp said, "Not nearly as hot as the fire you'll experience!"

The executioner lit the kindling. At first the flames leaped up around Polycarp, but didn't touch his body. Seeing this, the executioner took a spear and thrust him through. The blood that poured out extinguished the fire. The Christians took his body and gave him a Christian burial.

It is significant, in a church whose members should suffer persecution and tribulation and have many martyred, that even the bishop of the church was put to death. The early leader was not above the people he ministered to; he shared in the trials and sufferings with his flock.

Unto the angel of the church in Smyrna write; These things says the first and the last, which was dead, and is alive (Rev. 2:8).

Because they were to be martyred, Jesus is reminding these Christians of His triumph over death. "I am the resurrection, and the life: he that believes in Me, though he were dead, yet shall he live" (John 11:25). Jesus said, "Because I live, you shall live also" (John 14:19). By reminding them of His triumph over death, He's giving them courage and strength for the hour when they would be facing death.

To the church at Smyrna John was told to write: "I know your works, and tribulation, and poverty, (but you are rich)" (Rev. 2:9). This is in contrast to the church of Laodicea that said, "We are rich," but Jesus said, "You're poor."

The estimate of ourselves is one thing, but His estimate of us is far different. The estimate of the church of Smyrna of themselves was that of poverty. Jesus said, "You are rich." "Has not God chosen the poor of this world rich in faith?" (James 2:5).

"I know the blasphemy of them which say they are Jews, and are not, but are the synagogue of Satan" (Rev. 2:9). Most of the persecution that came in the early church was instigated and inspired by the Jews. Wherever Paul went, the Jews followed him and stirred up agitation in each city against him.

The term "Jew" refers to one who practices Judaism. It isn't a nationality. You can actually proselyte and become a Jew, that is, a worshiper of God through Judaism. Some Jews were *claiming* to be worshipers of God but they were not. They had their synagogues, but Jesus said of them that they were the synagogues of Satan.

The Jews said to Jesus, "We are of our father Abraham. Who your father is nobody knows." Jesus said, "If you are Abraham's children, then you would have believed in me, for Abraham testified of me." Jesus said, "You are of your father the devil, and you do his works" (John 8:31–47).

REVELATION 2:10-11

To the church of Smyrna He said, "Fear none of those things which you shall suffer. Behold, the devil shall cast some of you into prison" (Rev. 2:10). The Lord recognizes that Satan is behind all the persecution and tribulation of the church. Jesus said to His disciples, "In the world you shall have tribulation" (John 16:33). The devil works through people even as God works through people. We need to realize that Satan is behind the inspiration and works of many people.

"The devil shall cast some of you into prison, that you may be tried; and you shall have tribulation ten days." The "ten days" could refer to the ten great periods of tribulation under the Roman government. "Be faithful unto death, and I will give you a crown of life" (Rev. 2:10).

Jesus has nothing bad to say about the church of Smyrna. No call to repentance. Smyrna is the church that will be purified by persecution. They'll be martyred and experience great tribulation. Tribulation never hurt the church. It always had a purifying effect. Jesus is encouraging them to be faithful unto death and He will give them a crown of life.

There is the crown of life. There's also a crown of righteousness. Paul said,

There is laid up for me a crown of righteousness, which the Lord, the righteous Judge, shall give me at that day: and not to me only, but unto all them also that love his appearing (2 Timothy 4:8).

He who has an ear, let him hear what the Spirit says unto the churches; He who overcomes shall not be hurt by the second death (Rev. 2:11).

The second death is explained to us in Revelation 20, when all the world (excluding Christians) stands before the great white throne judgment of God. Death and hell will give up the dead. Whoever's name is not found written in the Lamb's Book of Life shall be cast into Gehenna, the second death.

Those who overcome shall not be hurt of the second death. "Blessed and holy is he," the Scripture said, "who has part in the first resurrection: on such the second death has no power" (Rev. 20:6).

When Jesus comes again to reign upon the earth and establishes His kingdom, Satan shall be bound for one thousand years and placed in the *abyss*. During this period Jesus will reign upon the earth in righteousness. The church will be reigning with Him as kings and priests. At the end of the thousand years, Satan will be loosed for a short season and will go throughout the world again to deceive the nations. He'll gather a great army to try to destroy Christ and to drive Him out of Jerusalem.

At times Christians come to me and say, "At the end of the thousand years, what if I'm deceived by Satan?" I answer, "Impossible!" "Blessed and holy is he that has part in the first resurrection: on such the second death has no power." You'll be in your new body, and there's no way you'll come into conspiracy with Satan at that time.

This short season will be a trial for those who have never had a trial as far as their Christian walk is concerned. Those who have been forced to live righteously during the kingdom age will be given an opportunity to do otherwise. The surprising thing is that so many will take it!

REVELATION 2:12-17

Pergamos—"And to the angel of the church in Pergamos write, These things says He who has the sharp sword with two edges, 'I know your works and where you dwell, even where Satan's seat [throne] is.'" The city of Pergamos was a city filled with sensuous worship of pagan deities.

"And you hold fast to My name, and have not denied My faith" (Rev. 2:12–13). A faithful remnant in this city of pagan worship is holding fast to the name of Jesus Christ. "Even in those days wherein Antipas was My faithful martyr, who was slain among you, where Satan dwells" (Rev. 2:13).

Jesus knows the works of the church of Pergamos—holding fast to His name in a pagan world, not denying the faith even at the martyrdom of Antipas, one of its members.

"But I have a few things against you, because you have there those that hold the doctrine of Balaam, who taught Balak to cast a stumbling block before the children of Israel, to eat things sacrificed unto idols, and to commit fornication" (Rev. 2:14).

The worship of these pagan deities was usually marked by the most abominable practices. The pagan temples had priestesses who were actually prostitutes, and the revenue for most of the pagan temples was gained through prostitution. Part of their religious rites involved sexual orgies with these priestesses.

In that area of Asia the Gnostics said that everything material was evil. Their belief was that God had nothing to do with the material world. Therefore, it didn't matter what you did to your body. They taught that you could do anything you wanted, because God wasn't concerned with your evil body. He was only concerned with your spirit. Thus, the Gnostics allowed all kinds of lasciviousness. Peter warned against this in his epistle (1 Peter 4:1–3).

In Pergamos some were saying, "We can do whatever we want! We're Christians and we're covered by grace. The body doesn't count, anyhow." Even though they were now professing Christians, they advocated worshiping in these pagan rites. This was the doctrine of Balaam—the worship of idols and committing fornication.

"Also you have those who hold the doctrine of the Nicolaitanes"—the establishment of a priesthood. Jesus said, "Which thing I hate." The Lord's word to them was, "Repent; or else I will come to you quickly, and will fight against them with the sword of My mouth" (Rev. 2:15–16).

He that has an ear, let him hear what the Spirit says unto the churches; to him that overcomes will I give to eat of the hidden manna, and will give him a white stone, and in the stone a new name written, which no man knows except he who receives it (Rev. 2:17).

The "hidden manna" is that life in Jesus Christ. He said, "I am the bread of life: he that comes to me shall never hunger" (John 6:35).

The "white stone" was actually the stone of acceptance or approval and was used in voting. A white stone signified a "yes" vote and a black stone a "no" vote. Some clubs have adopted a similar practice today. White or black balls are dropped into a ballot box whenever an applicant is considered for membership, and he is rejected, or black-balled," if someone drops in a black ball.

Jesus said that He will give us a white stone—"Accepted." I've been accepted by God in Christ. The white stone has "a new name written, which no man knows except he who receives it" (Rev. 2:17).

Two evils had begun to creep into the church—the introduction of idolatry and the introduction of a priesthood. The church of Pergamos historically is the development of the church-state system under Constantine in AD 316. It was the beginning of the Roman Catholic Church.

REVELATION 2:18-22

Thyatira—"And unto the angel of the church in Thyatira write; These things says the Son of God, who has eyes like a flame of fire, and His feet are like fine brass." "Brass" always symbolizes judgment in the Scriptures. "I know your works, and love, and service, and faith, and your patience, and your works; and the last to be more than the first" (Rev. 2:18–19).

This church had a lot of things going for it. Thyatira was one of the most active churches around. Works, love, service, faith, patience; tremendous characteristics, yet, the Lord said,

I have a few things against you, because you allow that woman Jezebel, who calls herself a prophetess, to teach and to seduce My servants to commit fornication, and to eat things sacrificed unto idols (Rev. 2:20).

That Jezebel system is the introduction of idolatry into the church and spiritual fornication. These things also took place with the nation Israel and, thus, Israel was rejected by God.

I gave her space to repent of her fornication and she repented not. Behold, I will cast her into a bed, and those who commit adultery with her into great tribulation, except they repent of their deeds (Rev. 2:21–22).

Is the church going to go through the great tribulation? I must answer, "Yes, a part of the church will be going through the great tribulation." The part of the church that does go through is the church of Thyatira, the woman Jezebel who failed to repent of her spiritual adultery and spiritual fornication.

Those who want to make a case of the church going through the tribulation—this is the case that they can make. The unrepentant church of Thyatira will go into the great tribulation.

When God, in the Ten Commandments, specifically forbid their making any images or likenesses of things in heaven above or on the earth beneath or in the water beneath, why do they adorn their churches with images of Jesus, Mary, or the saints?

REVELATION 2:23-29

"And I will kill her children with death; and all the churches shall know that I am He who searches the minds and hearts: and I will give unto every one of you according to your works. But unto you I say, and unto the rest in Thyatira, as many as have not this doctrine, and which have not known the depths of Satan, as they speak; I will put upon you none other burden. But that which you have already hold fast till I come. And he that overcomes, and keeps my works unto the end, to him will I give power over the nations: And he shall rule them with a rod of iron; as the vessels of a potter shall they be broken to shivers: even as I received of my Father. And I will give him the morning star. He who has an ear, let him hear what the Spirit says unto the churches" (Rev. 2:23–29).

The promise to the overcomers is that beautiful promise of ruling with a rod of iron in the Kingdom of God and being given the morning star, Jesus Christ. The rod of iron signifies the type of reign during the kingdom age. People will be forced to be good. Our duties as the church reigning with Christ will be to enforce His righteousness.

CHAPTER 3
THREE MESSAGES

REVELATION 3:1-6

Sardis—

And unto the angel of the church in Sardis write; These things says He who has the seven Spirits of God, and the seven stars; I know your works, that you have a name that you are alive, but you are dead. Be watchful, and strengthen the things which remain, that are ready to die: for I have not found your works perfect before God. Remember therefore how you have received and heard, and hold fast, and repent. If therefore you will not watch, I will come upon you as a thief, and you will not know what hour I will come upon you (Rev. 3:1-3).

Protestantism has a name that is alive but is dead. It's tragic what has happened to the Protestant churches. A great percentage of the ministers don't believe in the virgin birth of Jesus Christ. They don't believe in His atoning death. They don't believe in heaven or hell. They practically deny the faith. So many Protestant churches are just a social club and a social organization, the term "born again" is meaningless to them. They have a name that they're alive but really they're dead. The Lord encourages them to strengthen those things which are left, because He has not found their works complete.

One thing about the Protestant Reformation—it didn't reform enough. Actually, the Protestants continued to use the many pagan customs adopted by the churches of Pergamos and Thyatira. They still had infant baptism. They still had so many pagan symbols. They still had the pagan holidays. Their reformation was incomplete.

The Lord says, "I've not found your work complete before God. Remember how you received and heard? Hold fast and repent. If you will not watch, I will come as a thief and you'll not know what hour I will come." He's warning the Protestant churches of His coming; but if they're not watching for His coming, He'll come upon them as a thief. They'll be taken by surprise.

Jesus said that we should watch and be ready for we know not what hour our Lord will come (Matthew 24:42, 44). Paul the apostle said, "we are not the children of darkness that the day should overtake us as a thief, but we're children of light; therefore, walk as children of light" (Ephesians 5:8).

"You have a few names even in Sardis which have not defiled their garments; and they shall walk with me in white," the Lord said.

For they are worthy. He who overcomes, the same shall be clothed in white raiment and I will not blot out his name out of the Book of Life, but I will confess his name before my Father, and before His angels (Rev. 3:4–5).

What does Jesus mean about blotting names out of the Book of Life? He means just that. Don't think I'm going to take away from this book. For in the final chapter it says that if any man shall take away from this book, his name will be taken out of the Book of Life (Rev. 22:19). I don't want mine blotted out! You say, "What did He mean by that?" I don't know but I won't try to explain it away. "He who has an ear, let him hear what the Spirit says unto the churches" (Rev. 3:6).

REVELATION 3:7-13

Philadelphia—The church of Philadelphia is God's faithful church in the last days. God help us that we would be the church of Philadelphia.

To the angel of the church in Philadelphia write; These things says He who is holy, He who is true, He who has the key of David, He who opens, and no man shuts; and shuts, and no man opens. I know your works: behold, I have set before you an open door, and no man can shut it: for you have a little strength, and have kept my word, and have not denied my name (Rev. 3:7–8).

We're not really powerful. We have a little strength. Thank God for the little strength that we have. "You have kept my word." God help us to be faithful to the Word, to study the Word, and to keep the Word as the paramount issue within the church. And we've not denied the name of Jesus Christ; we've not denied Him and who He is.

Behold, I will make them of the synagogue of Satan, which say they are Jews, and are not, but do lie; behold, I will make them to come and worship before your feet, and to know that I have loved you (Rev. 3:9).

In the kingdom age the Jews will know that God has loved the Gentile church.

Because you have kept the word of my patience, I also will keep you from the hour of temptation, which shall come upon all the world, to try them that dwell upon the earth (Rev. 3:10).

Here is God's promise to the *faithful* church to keep them from the great tribulation. In Luke 21 Jesus said as He was talking of the events of the great tribulation, "Pray always, that you may be accounted worthy to escape all these things… and to stand before the Son of man" (Luke 21:36).

Behold, I come quickly: hold fast what you have, that no man take your crown. He who overcomes will I make a pillar in the temple of My God, and he shall go out no more: and I will write upon him the name of My God, and the name of the city of My God, which is New Jerusalem, which comes down out of heaven from My God: and I will write upon him My new name. He who has an ear, let him hear what the Spirit says unto the churches (Rev. 3:11-13).

This is the promise that we'll be a pillar in the temple of God. We will be actually a part of the kingdom age and rule and reign with Him in the New Jerusalem coming down from God out of heaven.

REVELATION 3:14-17

Laodicea—The church of Laodicea is the apostate church of the last days.

Write, "These things says the Amen, the faithful and true witness, the beginning of the creation of God" (Rev. 3:14).

In Revelation, Jesus is referred to as the true and faithful witness of God. "The beginning of the creation of God" the Greek does not signify that Jesus is a created being, but that He is the original cause of creation. For "all things were created by Him, and for Him: and He is before all things, and by Him all things consist" (Colossians 1:16–17). "All things were made by Him; and without Him was not any thing made that was made" (John 1:3). Jesus is the origination of the creation powers or the origin of God's creation. So He is actually the creative force, and that's what Revelation is speaking of here—the creative force of the creation of God.

> I know your works, that you are neither cold nor hot: I would that you were cold or hot. So then because you are lukewarm, and neither cold nor hot, I will spew you out of my mouth (Rev. 3:15–16).

The reason for the lukewarm conditions: 'Because you say, I am rich, and increased with goods, and have need of nothing" (Rev. 3:17). Their trust in materialism has brought them to a lukewarm state. "You cannot serve God and mammon" (Matthew 6:24). Mixing the two will lead you into becoming lukewarm.

"You know not that you are wretched, and miserable, and poor, and blind, and naked" (Rev. 3:17). The contrasting views—one was their own view about themselves, the other was God's view about them. Jesus said that you do err if you judge yourself by men (Luke 18:9–14). Many times we look around and judge ourselves by man's standard. We might think we're all right.

But man's standard isn't the standard by which we're to judge ourselves or by which we'll be judged. Jesus Christ is the standard. He demonstrates to us what God intended man to be. Hold yourself up next to Him and see how you look. That will give you an idea of what the true judgment will be like. If you say, "Well, I'm better than Chuck Smith"—that's not going to buy you anything!

Jesus said, "Except your righteousness shall exceed the righteousness of the scribes and Pharisees, you shall in no case enter into the kingdom of heaven" (Matthew 5:20). You'll never make it on your own righteousness. The only righteousness that is acceptable is the righteousness that God has imputed unto you by your faith in Jesus Christ. The righteousness that is of Christ through faith is the only way you'll get an entrance into the kingdom of heaven.

REVELATION 3:18-22

Those of Laodicea had their own opinion of themselves. The Lord had a different opinion of them. "I counsel you to buy from Me gold refined in the fire, that you may be rich; and white raiment, that you may be clothed, and that the shame of your nakedness do not appear; and anoint your eyes with eye salve, that you may see. As many as I love, I rebuke and chasten" (Rev. 3:18–19).

"My son, do not despise the chastening of the Lord ... for whom the Lord loves He chastens, and scourges every son whom He receives" (Hebrews 12:5–6). If you're not chastened then you're an illegitimate child. You're really not His son. God only chastens His sons. Don't get down on God when He chastens you. Rejoice! At least it proves you're His son. If He didn't care, He wouldn't even bother. This is His first cure for being lukewarm.

The second cure for lukewarmness: be zealous. Get out of that lukewarm rut. Get out of that tepid state. Become zealous for the Lord. The final cure for lukewarmness is to open your heart to God and repent. "Behold, I stand at the door, and knock: if any man hears My voice, and open the door, I will come in to him, and will sup with him [or eat supper with him], and he with Me" (Rev. 3:20).

The Lord is inviting Himself into the closest, deepest, most intimate communion and fellowship with you—eating together with you, partaking with each other, becoming a part of each other by supping together. "To him that overcomes will I grant to sit with Me in my throne" (Rev. 3:21). We'll be ruling with Christ and sitting by Him on His throne even as Jesus has been exalted and is sitting at the right hand of the throne of the Father on high. "He who has an ear, let him hear what the Spirit says unto the churches" (Rev. 3:22).

THE RAPTURE

REVELATION 4:1

Here we enter into the third division of the book of Revelation. Chapter 4 begins with the Greek phrase *meta tauta* or "after these things."

> After these things [the things of the church] I looked, and, behold, a door was opened in heaven: and the first voice which I heard was as it were of a trumpet talking with me; which said, Come up here, and I will show you things which must be hereafter [also *meta tauta*—'after these things'] (Rev. 4:1).

We have now come to the end of the church history upon the earth and the final message to the churches.

In His messages to the last four churches, Jesus spoke of His second coming. He warned the churches of His return. "Behold, I come quickly," He said. If they didn't repent they would be cast into the great tribulation. If they kept the word of His patience, Jesus promised that He would keep them from the hour of temptation.

"After these things"—after the church has finished her testimony upon the earth and God is through with us—there shall come from heaven,

> The voice of the archangel, and the trump of God: and the dead in Christ shall rise first: then we who are alive and remain shall be caught up together with them in the clouds, to meet the Lord in the air: and so shall we ever be with the Lord (1 Thessalonians 4:16–17).

The church will be transported into heaven for a seven-year period during which time there will be great tribulation upon the earth. (For an expanded commentary on the rapture of the church, see *The Rapture* by the author.)

After the church's witness and work upon the earth is completed, the trump of God shall sound. The trumpet sound will be saying to the Christians, the body of Christ, "Come up here!"

While in summer camp, I've heard the trumpet say "Rise and shine!" and I've heard the trumpet say "Go to bed." I've heard the trumpet say "Come and eat!", and at football games I've heard it say "Charge!" But I'm waiting for the trumpet to say "Come up here!" I don't know what kind of a trumpet call it will be—but I'll understand it and recognize it the minute I hear it!

When the trump of God shall sound, the dead will be raised incorruptible. And "we shall all be changed, in a moment, in the twinkling of an eye" (1 Corinthians 15:51–52), "caught up... to meet the Lord in the air: and so shall we ever be with the Lord" (1 Thessalonians 4:17). The Bible does not say that we shall be in heaven forever. It says that we shall be "with the Lord."

Wherever Jesus is, that's where everyone who is a Christian will be, because we're all part of the body of Christ. We'll never be separated from Him. While He is in heaven, we'll be in heaven. When He comes back to earth, we'll come back to the earth. When He goes into the new heaven and the new earth, we'll go into the new heaven and the new earth.

The Jehovah's Witnesses say, "I don't want to go to heaven and twiddle my thumbs for eternity." Born-again Christians don't intend to. We intend to be there for seven years while the earth goes through the tribulation. We'll enjoy the marriage supper of the Lamb in heaven. Then we expect to come back to reign with Christ upon the earth. We'll reign with Him as kingdom priests on the earth for one thousand years, then enter into the new heaven and new earth wherein dwells righteousness, and we'll live and reign with Him forever.

If the Lord told me to sit on a cloud and twiddle my thumbs, I'd be the happiest thumb-twiddler in all the universe! I'm not afraid of what God has in store for me. I can hardly wait! I'm sure it'll be more exciting than twiddling my thumbs. I feel sorry for those people who degrade heaven. They say, "You're always talking about the 'sweet by and by' or the 'pie in the sky.' You should be more concerned with the 'here and now'."

It was Jesus who encouraged us and gave us this glorious hope. I'm looking forward to going to heaven. I don't care what they say, I'm anxious to see it. Jesus said, "I go to prepare a place for you. And if I go and prepare a place for you, I will come again, and receive you unto myself; that where I am, there you may be also" (John 14:2–3). There's the clue. Where Jesus is, that's where I'll be, and in His presence is fullness of joy.

It took seven days for the Lord to create this beautiful world. He's been preparing heaven for two thousand years. Imagine what it must be like by now! And you don't want to go there? Friend, you can stay here in all this pollution if you want to, but I'm going up!

I believe that the rapture of the church takes place in verse one of Revelation 4—after the things of the church history are completed. John heard a voice as a trumpet saying, "Come up here, and I will show you things that shall be after these things." Now John will see the things that shall take place after the church is gone.

REVELATION 4:2-7

The Heavenly Scene—"And immediately I was in the spirit: and, behold, a throne was set in heaven, and One sat on the throne" (Rev. 4:2).

Why was John "in the spirit"? Because flesh and blood cannot enter the kingdom of heaven. "And One sat on the throne." This is the great, beautiful throne of God. As John looked at God, he didn't see any form.

"And He who sat was to look upon like a jasper and a sardius stone" (Rev. 4:3). Jasper is a diamond-like, clear, crystal stone with a purple hue. The sardius stone is blood red. The sardius stone was the first stone and the jasper stone was the last stone that the high priest in the Old Testament wore on his breastplate (Exodus 28:17–20). "And there was a rainbow round about the throne, in sight like unto an emerald" (Rev. 4:3).

John saw God sitting upon His throne in majesty on high. What an awesome sight this must have been! He saw the brilliance of God like the brilliance of the jasper and sardius stones—a mixture of clear, crystal, purplish hue with blood red—and an emerald green rainbow "round about the throne" of God.

"And round about the throne were twenty-four smaller seats." The word translated *seats* in the King James Bible is the Greek word for "thrones." "And upon the thrones I saw twenty-four elders sitting, clothed in white raiment; and they had on their heads crowns of gold" (Rev. 4:4).

There are many Bible expositors who believe that the twenty-four elders are actually representative of the church. They have white robes, as does the church in Revelation 19:8, which is the righteousness of the saints. The twenty-four elders also have crowns of gold upon their heads. We the church have been promised the crowns of life, the crowns of righteousness by our Lord. Many Bible expositors see the elders representing the church on its throne, ruling and reigning with Christ in heaven. This is a very possible interpretation.

It is also possible that these elders represent the saints from the Old and the New Testaments—the twelve tribes and the twelve apostles. It is also possible that they're created beings of God like angels and cherubs. These elders may be created beings for the specific ministry of sitting on the twenty-four thrones around God's throne. We cannot know for sure.

And out of the throne proceeded lightnings and thunderings and voices: and there were seven lamps of fire burning before the throne, which are the seven Spirits of God (Rev. 4:5).

Again, I refer you to Isaiah 11:2 for the seven-fold working of the Holy Spirit in Jesus Christ (see Rev. 1:4 commentary).

And before the throne there was a sea of glass like unto crystal: and in the midst of the throne, and round about the throne, were four beasts [proper translation is "living creatures"] (Rev. 4:6).

These are not beasts like wild or dumb animals; they are actually highly intelligent created beings of God. As they are described in and compared with Ezekiel 1 and 10, we know that these are cherubim about the throne of God.

These four living creatures were "full of eyes before and behind. The first living creature was like a lion, and the second was like a calf, and the third had a face as a man, and the fourth was like a flying eagle" (Rev. 4:6–7).

Some see these creatures as manifestations of Christ in the Gospels. In the first Gospel, Matthew presents Jesus as the **lion** of the tribe of Judah. Mark presents Him as a **calf**, a beast of burden representing a suffering servant. Luke presents Him as the Son of **man**. John presents Him as the Son of God, the **eagle** representing the Divinity.

REVELATION 4:8-11

And the four living creatures had each of them six wings about him; and they were full of eyes within: and they rest not day and night, saying, Holy, holy, holy, Lord God Almighty, which was, and is, and is to come. And when those living creatures give glory and honor and thanks to Him who sat on the throne, who lives for ever and ever, the twenty-four elders fall down before Him who sat on the throne, and they worship Him that lives for ever and ever, and cast their crowns before the throne, saying, Your are worthy, O Lord, to receive glory and honor and power: for You have created all things, and for Your pleasure they are and were created (Rev. 4:8–11).

Here we get a view of the heavenly scene. Study Revelation 4. Fix it in your mind. You don't want to look like a country bumpkin on his first trip to the big city when you get to heaven. You don't want to be looking around and asking everyone, "What's that!?"

You'll see God sitting upon the throne with the emerald rainbow about the throne. You'll see the twenty-four lesser thrones for the elders and you'll see the cherubim who stand before God continually saying, "Holy, holy, holy, Lord God Almighty, which was, and is, and is to come"—declaring the holiness and eternal character of God. As they do this, the twenty-four elders fall down upon the crystal sea which is before the throne of God, cast their crowns before the throne, and declare God's worthiness to receive their worship. God is worthy by virtue of the fact that He has created all things and that all things were made for Him and for His pleasure.

Now, like it or not, God created you for His own pleasure. You say, "I don't think it's fair!" Well, that's tough. That's the way it is. Like it or not, that's why you've been created.

If you truly submit to that scriptural truth, you'll find fulfillment. If you don't submit to it, you'll go around forever empty, always frustrated, and ever reaching out for something more, but never finding satisfaction. Since God created you for His pleasure, the only way your life will be meaningful and fulfilling is by bringing pleasure to God.

"Without faith it is impossible to please God: for he that comes to God must believe that He is, and that He is a rewarder of them that diligently seek Him" (Hebrews 11:6). When you diligently seek after God, you bring Him pleasure. The way to have fulfillment is to live a life of faith seeking after full fellowship with God. You'll find the most satisfying and complete life you can have when you're fulfilling the basic reason for God creating of you.

"You are worthy, O Lord, to receive glory and honor and power: for You have created all things, and for Your pleasure they are and were created." All things were created for God's good pleasure. A lot of people come down on God for this. That's their problem. You can fight against it if you want but you won't get anywhere. The best thing is to submit to it. You can fight against a block wall to get through it. You can beat yourself against it all you want, but I happen to know what's in a block wall. I've watched them put in the steel bars and pour the grout. I know that, try as you may, you'll only hurt yourself. You're not going to affect that wall one bit. You might stain it a bit with your blood, but that won't hurt it.

Likewise, you may fight against God all you want, but you're the one who's going to suffer. Your fighting doesn't take anything away from God. It's time you wake up and quit fighting against God.

CHAPTER 5
WHO OWNS THE EARTH?

REVELATION 5:1-7

I saw in the right hand of Him that sat on the throne [in the right hand of God] a book written within and on the backside, sealed with seven seals (Rev. 5:1).

The word *book* in the King James Version is better translated as "scroll" from the Greek.

And I saw a strong angel proclaiming with a loud voice, Who is worthy to open the scroll, and to loose the seals thereof? And no man in heaven, nor in earth, neither under the earth, was able to open the scroll, neither to look thereon. And I wept much, because no man was found worthy to open and to read the scroll, neither to look thereon (Rev. 5:2–4).

The Father is sitting upon the throne. In His right hand there is a scroll. It has writing on the inside and on the outside and is sealed with seven seals. An angel proclaims with a strong voice, "Who is worthy to take this scroll and to break the seals?" Because no one is found worthy in heaven or earth to take it, John begins to sob convulsively.

What is the scroll? What are the seals? What is their significance? This scroll must be the title deed of the earth.

When God created the earth He gave it to man, who was in the Garden of Eden. God said, "Be fruitful, and multiply, and replenish the earth" (Genesis 1:28). He placed man in Eden to dress the garden and to keep it. God gave man one restriction: don't eat of the tree in the midst of the garden, the tree of knowledge of good and evil. God said, "The day that you eat thereof you shall surely die" (Genesis 2:17).

We don't know how long man dwelt in the garden. But one day Satan came, tempted Eve, and she ate. She gave to Adam and he ate. They forfeited their right to the earth to Satan who had deceived and tempted them.

> Do you not know, that to whom you yield yourselves servants to obey, his servants you are to whom you obey; whether of sin unto death, or of obedience unto righteousness? (Romans 6:16).

By yielding themselves to the suggestion of Satan (eating of the forbidden fruit), they acted doubly. It was a disobedience to God, which took them out of fellowship with God, but it was also an obedience to Satan, which brought them into submission to Satan. At that point man forfeited the right to the earth. The title deed of the earth was passed over to Satan, and the world became Satan's.

Jesus came to redeem the world back to God—to buy the "field."

> The kingdom of heaven is like unto treasure hid in a field; which when a man found, he hid, and for joy over it goes and sells all that he has, and buys that field (Matthew 13:44).

The "treasure" in the field is the church.

Jesus died to purchase the earth. It was God's to begin with. God created it, but He gave it to man. Man, in turn, forfeited it to Satan, and Satan has been the ruler of the world ever since.

When Jesus came, Satan took Him up to a high mountain and showed Him all the kingdoms of the earth. Satan said, "All these things will I give You [for they are mine and I can give them to whomever I will], if You will fall down and worship me" (Matthew 4:9). Satan claimed as his own the kingdoms of the world and the power to give them over to Jesus Christ—if Jesus would only bow and worship him.

Jesus did not dispute Satan's claim. It was a valid claim. The kingdoms of the world belonged to Satan. Don't blame God for the starvation in the world today. Don't blame God for deformed babies.

Don't blame God for wars and crimes. These have come as the result of man's rebellion against God. You don't see God's order in the world today. You see Satan's order. He's the prince of the world.

Jesus, in referring to Satan, said to His disciples, "The prince of this world is coming, and has nothing in Me" (John 14:30). Paul called Satan "the god of this world." We see the world under Satan's control. "The god of this world has blinded the minds of them which believe not" (2 Corinthians 4:4). Thank God that He chose us in His love and opened our eyes to His truth so we might come into His kingdom!

Jesus came to redeem the world back to God. He paid the price of redemption when He died for us upon the cross. We are redeemed not with corruptible things such as silver and gold from the former life but with the precious blood of Jesus Christ (1 Peter 1:18–19). Jesus bought the world, but He has not yet taken possession of it.

God has placed all things in subjection under Him, but we do not yet see all things in subjection to Him (1 Peter 1:18–19). Though Jesus purchased the world, He has not yet taken the title deed to it and claimed that which He has purchased. He's going to do that very soon.

A very interesting Jewish law is encountered here—the law of the forfeiture of property. If you as a Jew lost your property by forfeit, it remained with the new owner for a period of years. In the appointed year you had the right to purchase your property back as long as you could fulfill the requirements that were written in the scroll which was sealed.

Under Jewish law, if you yourself couldn't redeem your property, a relative or near of kin could step in and redeem it. This way the property remained in the family. If your relative did redeem it, he would be known as the goel (in Hebrew) or "kinsman redeemer."

Now, if in the seventh year no one was able to redeem the property, then it would remain under the new ownership; but you never totally lost ownership until this redemption period was over, and you or the kinsman redeemer were unable to fulfill the requirements of redemption.

On the other hand, if you could redeem it, you would call for the elders of the city to meet with you before the city gates. You would bring out the scroll that had all the requirements upon it and you would break the seal. You'd open the scroll and show your ability to pay the price, proving that you had the right to redeem it. You could actually purchase the property back for yourself in that year of redemption. Likewise, if you were sold into slavery, you would remain a slave for six years, but the seventh year you would be set free. This was the Jewish law of redemption—being set free.

This law is significant because man was sold into the slavery of sin about six thousand years ago. The right of redemption will soon be up. Satan has possessed this place for about six thousand years, and we're about to enter the seventh thousand-year era very soon. This will be the millennial reign of Christ as God redeems that which He purchased through the blood of Jesus Christ.

Man through the years has been trying to figure out exactly when the six thousand years will come to an end. We cannot know for sure, but we know we're getting close. "No man knows the day or the hour" (Matthew 24:36).

In the heavenly scene of Revelation 5 this "scroll" is the title deed of the earth. The time has come, the six thousand years have expired, and the angel proclaimed with a strong voice, "Who is worthy to take the scroll? Who can purchase the world back from Satan?" No man was found worthy. No man can redeem himself, much less the world.

John said that when no one was found worthy, he began to sob convulsively. Why? Because it meant that the world would go on forever in Satan's power and control. Such a thing was unthinkable in the mind of John.

We see the world today and the tragic results of man's submission to Satan's authority—the sicknesses, the sorrows, and the sufferings. To think that we would have to go on forever in this condition would indeed be a sad thing.

But "one of the elders said, Weep not: behold, the Lion of the tribe of Judah, the Root of David, has prevailed to open the book, and to loose the seven seals thereof" (Rev. 5:5). John turned and "in the midst of the throne and of the four living creatures, and in the middle of the elders, stood a Lamb as it had been slain, having seven horns and seven eyes, which are the seven Spirits of God sent forth into all the earth. And He came and took the book out of the right hand of Him that sat upon the throne" (Rev. 5:7).

John sees the Lion of the tribe of Judah take the book to loose the seals. However, John saw Him not as a lion; he saw Jesus as a lamb that had been slain. Evidently, the marks of the crucifixion are still upon Christ when He is in heaven in glory.

We know that after His resurrection Jesus had the marks of the cross in His hands and feet. It is possible that He still had the marks of the buffeting upon His face, because the disciples didn't recognize Him. Mary didn't recognize Him in the garden; she thought He was the gardener. The two disciples on the road to Emmaus didn't recognize Him. His face may have been disfigured. It may be so even in heaven, for John sees Him as a lamb that had been slain.

Isaiah, prophetically looking forward, said, "Who has believed our report? And to whom is the arm of the LORD revealed?" (Isaiah 53:1). Isaiah speaks of seeing Christ and the shock we'll have at seeing Him. "There's no beauty in Him that we should desire Him" (Isaiah 53:2). It's very possible that, when we first see Christ, He'll still be bearing the marks of His suffering. Isaiah said that as many as looked at Him were astonished because His face was so marred (Isaiah 52:14). Jesus could not be recognized as a man because of the beating that He took.

It's a heavy thought to think that Jesus might still be bearing these marks for our sins. We may see them as a reminder of God's love for us, and our hearts will go out to Jesus because He suffered so much for us. We shall ultimately see Him in His glory when He returns with His church to reign over the earth.

Isaiah also speaks about the astonishment of seeing Satan. They shall be astonished who look upon Lucifer, saying, "Is this the one who created all that trouble on the earth and gave me such a bad time?" (Isaiah 14:10–19). I think we'll be astonished when we see Satan because of his intense beauty—one of the most beautiful beings created by God.

REVELATION 5:8-14

John saw Jesus, as a lamb that had been slain, in the midst of the throne, in the midst of the living creatures, and in the midst of the twenty-four elders. Jesus took the scroll out of the right hand of Him that sat upon the throne. Immediately, all heaven breaks forth in chorus shouts of praises and victory.

> When he had taken the scroll, the four living creatures and the twenty-four elders fell down before the Lamb, having every one of them harps, and golden vials full of odors, which are the prayers of saints (Rev. 5:8).

How many times have you prayed, "Thy kingdom come. Thy will be done in earth, as it is in heaven"? We're still waiting for that prayer to be fulfilled. It was the first of the petitions Jesus said we should pray. "After this manner, therefore, pray: Our Father which art in heaven, Hallowed be thy name." That's worship and ascribing glory to God. But then "Thy kingdom come. Thy will be done" (Matthew 6:9–10). The first of all our petitions should be that desire for God's coming kingdom. That should be the paramount desire of our hearts and lives.

At this time in Revelation, our prayers are being brought forth as incense before God in these golden vials. The time for the answer of this prayer is come.

And they sang a new song, saying, You are worthy to take the book, and to open the seals thereof: for You were slain, and have redeemed us to God by Your blood out of every kindred, and tongue, and people, and nation; and have made us unto our God kings and priests: and we shall reign on the earth (Rev. 5:9–10).

Look at that song. Look at the lyrics of that song. Who is singing it? Who can sing this to Jesus Christ? Only the church can sing that song. It isn't the song of Israel. They're not redeemed from all the nations. The church is taken out of all the nations. The church is the one that was redeemed and purchased by the blood of Jesus Christ.

Notice where the church is. It is in heaven singing this song when Jesus takes the scroll out of the right hand of God. When our prayers are offered as incense we break out in glorious song to Jesus. "Worthy is the Lamb…"

This is before the first seal, which initiates the great tribulation period upon the earth, is even opened. The church will not go through the tribulation. We'll be in heaven singing of the worthiness of Jesus Christ to take the scroll and to loose the seals. I plan to be there and I've already memorized the song. I don't have the tune yet, but I'll pick it up in a hurry. Thank God I can sing the song of redemption through the blood of Jesus Christ!

And I beheld, and I heard the voice of many angels round about the throne and the living creatures and the elders: and the number of them was ten thousand times ten thousand, and thousands of thousands (Rev. 5:11).

One hundred million and millions more are around the throne. Oh, what a great congregation that will be!

Saying with a loud voice, Worthy is the Lamb that was slain to receive power, and riches, and wisdom, and strength, and honor, and glory, and blessing (Rev. 5:12).

The angels of heaven worship Jesus Christ. God has said, "Let all the angels of God worship Him" (Hebrews 1:6). To hear one hundred million plus millions saying "Worthy is the Lamb" will be heavenly glory!

> And every creature which is in heaven, and on the earth, and under the earth, and such as are in the sea and all that are in them, I heard saying, Blessing, and honor, and glory, and power, be unto Him who sits upon the throne, and unto the Lamb for ever and ever (Rev. 5:13).

Here the Father and the Son are given equal glory and equal worship by all creation. "And the four living creatures said, Amen. And the twenty-four elders fell down and worshiped Him who lives for ever and ever" (Rev. 5:14).

This is the glorious heavenly scene when Jesus takes the scroll, the title deed of the earth, and begins the culmination of the work of redemption—laying claim to that which He has redeemed. This is what all creation is waiting for! Paul the apostle said, "For we know that the whole creation groans and travails in pain... waiting for the adoption, to wit, the redemption of our body" (Romans 8:22–23). In Revelation 5 Jesus claims His purchased possession. He takes the scroll and begins to take authority over that which is rightfully His.

CHAPTER 6

BAD NEWS

R evelation chapter six describes the events that will be taking place during the seven-year period upon the earth known as the great tribulation—from the time that Jesus takes His church out at the rapture until He comes again with His church at His glorious second coming described in Revelation 19. So, between Revelation 6 and 19 we have a detailed account of the horrors, destruction, and desolation coming to this old planet earth.

REVELATION 6:1-2

In Revelation chapter six Jesus begins to loose the seven seals in heaven, and we see the resultant events that take place upon the earth. "And I saw when the Lamb opened one of the seals, and I heard, as it were the noise of thunder, one of the four beasts [living creatures]" (Rev. 6:1).

The word *beast* is an unfortunate translation. To us *beast* denotes a dumb animal, but these are living creatures. These are angels called "cherubim" which are about the throne of God. They are a very intelligent creation of God.

One of the four living creatures said,

Come and see [the words "and see" are not in the earliest versions]. And I saw, and behold a white horse: and he that sat on him had a bow; and a crown was given unto him: and he went forth conquering, and to conquer (Rev. 6:1–2).

There are some who teach that the white horse rider is none other than Jesus Christ. I personally believe that the white horse rider is the Antichrist. I believe that the moment Jesus takes the church out of the world, the hindering force of the Holy Spirit will be removed—and then that man of sin shall be revealed, the son of perdition (2 Thessalonians 2:3, 7–8).

The power of God's Spirit working in the church is hindering the Antichrist from taking over the world today. Once the church is raptured, there'll be no hindering force whatsoever and the Antichrist will move in.

I also do not believe that this is the second coming of Jesus Christ because it is followed by wars, famines, and death. The coming of Jesus Christ will usher in the glorious era of peace—God's millennial age upon the earth. In addition, this white horse rider appears at the very beginning of the tribulation period; I cannot see this as the coming of Jesus Christ.

The term "conquering and to conquer" does speak of a ultimate conquest. The Antichrist will take over the earth and establish his kingdom. He'll receive the authority, throne, and kingdoms from Satan, which Satan once offered to Jesus if Jesus would bow to him, and begin his rule upon the earth.

It is interesting that we already see signs of the Antichrist in the world. I believe the "peace symbol" is one of the signs of the Antichrist. Historically, it is the sign of the broken inverted cross that originated with Caesar Nero. Nero is my candidate for the Antichrist (see Rev. 17:10–11 commentary). He originated this peace symbol as a sign of his hatred against Christianity.

The Bible declares that a powerful man will arise on the world scene. This man will bring the world under his control through a peace program and economic strategy.

The Antichrist will set up an economic system that will do away with money. Everyone will be assigned a mark. You won't be able to buy or sell without that mark. Ultimately, it will be affixed either in your hand or in your forehead (Rev. 13:16).

The Bible described this system two thousand years ago. In October 1974 in the state of California, several banks introduced what they called the "cashless society." You can pay your bills and arrange all your transactions by a bank number. The bank takes care of everything. You don't even need to see your paycheck. The bank receives it automatically from your employer.

Money has become a dangerous commodity because it's so easy to steal. Many service stations prefer customer to use a credit card or debit card to buy gas rather than cash.

Daniel tells us that the Antichrist will make a covenant with the nation Israel, which will no doubt grant her the right to rebuild the temple. However, after three and a half years the Antichrist will break this covenant with Israel, and in that rebuilt temple he'll set up an image of himself. This image has the power to speak and all the world will be ordered to worship it (Rev. 13).

We could theorize about the image with the capacity to speak and the numbering monetary system. You could say that the image is perhaps a fantastic computer system that will sit in the temple, and that all commerce will be done strictly through computer transactions and everybody will be assigned a number.

We can only guess how it will happen. However, it will happen. God's Word cannot fail. Jesus said, "Heaven and earth shall pass away, but My words shall not pass away" (Matthew 24:35). You can be sure, since God said it, that it's going to happen! This man of sin, the son of perdition, the Antichrist shall be revealed.

Satan, who rules over the earth at the present time, will give the Antichrist his throne. Satan will turn it over to this madman until the world is brought under his dominion, power, and control.

REVELATION 6:3-4

And when He had opened the second seal, I heard the second cherubim [living creature] say, Come. And there went out another horse that was red: and power was given to him that sat thereon to take peace from the earth, and that they should kill one another: and there was given unto him a great sword (Rev. 6:3–4).

The Antichrist will come first of all with the program of peace. He's going to establish himself as a "man of peace." He will actually be able to effect a certain degree of peace upon the earth for a time.

For the first three and a half years people will rejoice in the economic prosperity and peace that this man brings. They'll say, "Peace and safety! Let's eat, drink, and be merry! He's a genius! He's a god!" The world will begin to worship him. But his peace will be short-lived. Just as the people begin to say, "Peace and safety; then sudden destruction comes upon them" (1 Thessalonians 5:3).

The second horse, the red horse of war, comes and the world is plunged into great wars and conflicts which will culminate in the battle of Armageddon.

REVELATION 6:5-8

> When He had opened the third seal, I heard the third cherubim [living creature] say, Come. And I beheld, and lo a black horse; and he that sat on him had a pair of balances in his hand. And I heard a voice in the midst of the four living creatures say, A measure of wheat for a penny, and three measures of barley for a penny; and do not harm the oil and the wine (Rev. 6:5–6).

A "measure of wheat" is about a quart; "a penny" is a day's wage.

Jesus told a parable about the man who went out early in the morning to hire laborers to work in his fields, and he contracted them for a penny, a day's wage (Matthew 20:1–2). Today this amounts to approximately seventy-five to a hundred dollars.

Therefore, a measure or quart of wheat for a day's wage speaks of a famine or a scarcity of food. We know that prices are governed by the supply and demand of an item. Here they'll be selling a quart of wheat for forty-five dollars.

A lot of people are trying to hedge for the future by buying silver and gold. When it gets right down to the basics, the commodity that will really hold its value is food. You can't eat gold or silver. It doesn't digest well. So, if you want to be wise, put your money into wheat, and when this time comes you can be the wealthiest man during the tribulation period. But then, what are you going to do with the gold you get for the wheat?

There will be a tremendous famine upon the earth. In giving the signs of His coming to His disciples, Jesus spoke of famines, pestilences, and earthquakes being upon the earth (Matthew 24:7). We have famines already to a certain degree, and it's difficult to distribute the food to where it's needed because of wars and factions. It's very tragic in this day of modern industry and technology that man cannot even provide for the food needs of the world. And with the rapidly increasing population, things are getting worse—not better.

This famine follows in the wake of war. Should we have a nuclear war right now, the whole balance of food supply would be in a precarious position. Two-thirds of the world today is living under starvation conditions. There are very few nations that have a surplus of food. Imagine what would happen if a full-scale nuclear war was fought and all the food supplies became contaminated and inedible. We can easily see the possibility of a terrible famine coming upon the earth.

> When He had opened the fourth seal, I heard the voice of the fourth living creature [or cherubim] say. Come. And I looked, and behold a pale horse: and his name that sat on him was Death, and Hell followed with him. And power was given unto them over the fourth part of the earth, to kill with the sword, and with hunger, and with death, and with the beasts of the earth (Rev. 6:7–8).

The fourth horse rider comes forth, the pale horse of death. Through the wars (the red horse), through the famines (the black horse), and through this pale horse of death, one-quarter of the earth's population will be wiped out. As the earth's population is over six billion, over one billion people will be destroyed by these horsemen. It's hard for us to conceive of such carnage.

REVELATION 6:9-11

> And when He had opened the fifth seal, I saw under the altar the souls of them that were slain for the word of God, and for the testimony which they held: And they cried with a loud voice, saying, How long, O Lord, holy and true, will you not judge and avenge our blood on them that dwell on the earth? And white robes were given unto every one of them; and it was said unto them, that they should rest yet for a little season, until their fellow servants also and their brethren, that should be killed as they were, should be fulfilled (Rev. 6:9–11).

Who are these "souls" under the altar? They are those who were slain for the Word of God and for the testimony which they held. These are the souls who have been martyred during the tribulation period. They are calling for vengeance upon those who killed them.

These souls under the altar are not the church or church martyrs. The church has already taken its place in the heavenly scene, singing glory to the Lamb for the redemption by His blood (Rev. 5). This group martyred during the Tribulation period doesn't take its place in the heavenly scene until Revelation 7 (between the sixth and seventh seals).

Martyrs and the Mark—The Antichrist is going to make an image of himself, and the false prophet will demand that the earth worship this image (Rev. 13). These two have the power to put to death anyone who refuses to worship this image (Rev. 13:15). However, an angel is going to fly through the midst of the heaven saying unto the people, "Don't take the mark of the beast. Don't worship him or his image. If any man worships his image, there is no hope and he is condemned to Gehenna" (Rev. 14:9–11). There is no possibility of salvation for anyone who takes the mark of the beast, worships the beast, or worships his image. Many will refuse to take the mark and will turn to Jesus Christ.

Many will be killed during this time for the Word of God and the testimony they hold. Oftentimes we worry about the salvation of our loved ones. The worry is good. Perhaps you'll intercede and pray for them now. It's very important.

Once the church has been raptured, it doesn't mean that the opportunities of salvation have ceased. It will be possible for people to be saved during this great tribulation period. After the church has been taken out, many of your loved ones who have rejected Jesus Christ will know that your witness to them was true. I believe many of them will turn unto the Lord and seek salvation. God is gracious and merciful, and salvation will be given to those who will believe and trust in Him in that day.

These martyrs who have refused to take the mark of the beast are given white robes and told to rest for a short season until their total number be complete—until those to be slain as the martyrs were slain are fulfilled.

Some of you may be breathing a sigh of relief, saying, "If I miss the rapture I can always make it in the back door. I'll be one of the martyred souls under the altar." It would seem to me that if you have difficulty living for Christ now with the strength and help of the Holy Spirit, you'll have a harder time dying for Christ then. When the church is removed, you'll be on your own. It's much better to go in the rapture of the church.

REVELATION 6:12-14

And I beheld when He had opened the sixth seal, and, lo, there was a great earthquake; and the sun became black as sackcloth of hair, and the moon became as blood; and the stars of heaven fell unto the earth, even as a fig tree casts her untimely figs, when she is shaken of a mighty wind. And the heaven departed as a scroll when it is rolled together; and every mountain and island were moved out of their places (Rev. 6:12–14).

Great cataclysmic events will take place upon the earth, including great meteorite showers.

In Arizona there is a huge meteorite crater in the desert between Flagstaff and Winslow. One meteorite can do an amazing amount of damage. Imagine the devastation if such a meteorite hit an area like Los Angeles.

In 1908, a meteorite hit Siberia and leveled forests for miles. In fact, the explosion and the damage were so tremendous that the physicists believe the meteorite might have been anti-matter. Anti-matter in theory is a reversal of matter as we know it. Matter is composed of atoms having electrons revolving around a nucleus of protons. The theory of anti-matter proposes that antimatter atoms have protons revolving around a nucleus of electrons. According to this theory, when matter meets with anti-matter, there is a tremendous nuclear explosion. So devastating was the destruction in 1908 in Siberia, that some physicists have theorized an antimatter meteorite actually hit the earth. We don't know for sure.

It is interesting that Isaiah describes the same cataclysmic events as John. He said the earth will stagger to and fro like a drunken man and be moved out of its place (Isaiah 13:13; 24:20). Joel describes these things as he speaks about the powers of the heavens being shaken and the sun and the moon being darkened (Joel 2:30–31; 3:15–16). Jesus spoke about these great cataclysmic events as preceding His second coming.

There is an interesting book by Immanuel Velikovsky called *Worlds in Collision.* The major premise of this book is that the planet Venus was introduced into our solar system during the historic period of man. The author believes that Venus made a very close pass to the earth about the time that the children of Israel were delivered from the Egyptian bondage. It made its second pass at the time Joshua came into the Promised Land. Then the planet Venus was fixed in its present orbit in our solar system.

Velikovsky describes the events that took place at the time of Moses and the exodus from Egypt—those plagues that came upon the Egyptians when the waters turned to blood (Matthew 24:29–30). He ties these events in with the approach of the planet Venus to the earth and the myriad of meteorites that would result from this close pass. He speaks of the earth changing direction in its orbit at that point. He gives evidence to show that perhaps Venus' pass took place during this period of history, collaborating it with historic events around the world.

As Velikovsky described the events that would take place at the introduction of a planet into our solar system, my mind went on to the future and to an event that is going to happen—the great earthquake.

The sun becomes black and the stars of heaven (the meteorite showers) come upon the earth. There will be tremendous devastation. The heavens will depart as a scroll when it is rolled together, and every mountain and island will move out of its place. These are the cataclysmic judgments of God that will take place upon the earth at that time. Just how God is going to do it, we don't know—but He will do it.

Polar Axis Shift—We have another possible explanation for the predicted cataclysmic events. According to many physicists a polar axis shift takes place about every five thousand years. We're a little overdue for our polar axis shift now.

Our present polar axis is set at a twenty-three degree pitch in its relationship to the sun. This slant gives the earth its seasons. We know that the seasons today are not as they have always been. At one time there were forests at the South Pole. Explorers have discovered charcoal deposits two hundred feet under the ice.

The North Pole regions and Siberia used to be tropical areas. The remains of mammoths have been found encased in ice and perfectly preserved. This speaks of an "instant freeze" process taking place some time in the past. In the digestive tracts of these mammoths they have discovered tropical vegetation. So, we know that at one time the earth was actually more tropical and lush than it is now.

Physicists tell us that a polar axis shift creates great convulsions throughout the earth causing mountains to disappear. There used to be a great ocean around Salt Lake City, Utah. The Great Salt Lake is all that remains now. There are sea shell fossils at the south rim of the Grand Canyon. That whole area was once under a great sea. Some scientists believe that at the last polar axis shift this ocean covering Utah and Arizona actually flooded south, creating the Grand Canyon, and now comprises the Gulf of California.

During a polar axis shift whole mountain ranges disappear while others are forced upward, oceans move and tidal waves are generated. All the earth's geographical structure and surface undergoes tremendous change.

Before the earth changes the tilt of its axis, it goes into a wobble like a top that is slowly running down. Then it suddenly shifts. Studies by physicists show that the earth has already gone into a wobble and could shift at any time.

It is an interesting possibility and may be what Isaiah was referring to when he said, "The earth shall stagger to and fro like a drunken man [the wobble] and then shall be removed out of her place." God could shift the earth so that it receives an even, all around exposure to the sun. If the earth didn't have the present tilt, but was perpendicular to the sun we'd have the same uniform relationship to the sun and, once again, the polar caps would melt. The increased heat would produce much more moisture in the atmosphere, creating lush and tropical jungles all around the world.

It is very possible that the flood in Noah's time could have been created by the polar axis shift. It would closely correspond to the time some physicists say the last shift took place. This could also explain why the life span was shortened after the flood. The drastic atmospheric changes may have caused an increase in ultraviolet and infrared ray penetration and, consequently, a quickening of the aging process. It's quite interesting to study these scientific matters and to realize how marvelous a book God's Word, the Bible, actually is.

REVELATION 6:15-17

Will communism conquer the world? I can declare to you that it shall not, because we find different classes of men described in Revelation 6:15.

The kings of the earth, and the great men, and the rich men, and the chief captains, and the mighty men, and every bondman, and every free man [all classes of men that exist at the present time], hid themselves in the dens and in the rocks of the mountains; And said to the mountains and rocks, Fall on us, and hide us from the face of Him who sits on the throne, and from the wrath of the Lamb: For the great day of His wrath is come; and who shall be able to stand? (Rev. 6:15–17).

We are now living in the Age of Grace. God has been merciful and gracious unto us. God has been very longsuffering and patient. But the day of His wrath is coming.

God was long-suffering and patient with the men of Noah's day, waiting 120 years as Noah built the ark before the flood finally descended. The patience of God was manifested then, and God has been patient and long-suffering now. But God said in the time of Noah "My spirit shall not always strive with man" (Genesis 6:3). That is also true today.

There are many people who misinterpret the longsuffering of God for weakness. They say that God will not judge His people. David declared that the wicked who are rich and prosperous say, "Does God see? Does God hear? Will He judge the world?" (Psalm 94:7, 9). They live as if there were no God. But the day of God's wrath shall come—the tragic day for those who are left here.

The very fact that "the great day" is the day of God's wrath, "the wrath of the Lamb," would again preclude the church being upon the earth. "For God has not appointed us to wrath" (1 Thessalonians 5:9).

When the wrath of God was to be poured out upon the cities of Sodom and Gomorrah, Abraham said unto the Lord, "Will not the Lord of the earth be just? Isn't God fair? Would You destroy the righteous with the wicked?" And Abraham proposed, "What if there be fifty righteous in the city, would You destroy the fifty righteous?"

The answer was, "No." If there were fifty righteous men then God would spare the city for their sake. But what if there's only forty-five righteous? He'd still spare it. What if there were only thirty? He'd still spare it. What if there were only ten? God would still spare it. But when the angel of the Lord arrived in the city of Sodom, there were not ten righteous. So, the Lord delivered Lot and his wife and two daughters (Lot's wife didn't make it completely). Then the judgment came upon the cities of Sodom and Gomorrah (1 Thessalonians 5:9).

God delivers the righteous. Referring to this very same incident, Peter said, "The Lord knows how to deliver the godly out of temptations, and to reserve the unjust unto the day of judgment to be punished" (2 Peter 2:9).

The day of God's wrath is coming. But God isn't angry with us, for we have accepted His provision through Jesus Christ. God's anger against our sin was visited upon Jesus Christ, and He died in our place.

CHAPTER 7
TWO SPECIAL GROUPS

A fter Revelation 6 there's a break. Revelation 7 is a parenthetical chapter. We stop the chronological progression while John introduces some other events before the scroll's seventh seal is opened. We're introduced first to a group of people whose number is 144,000.

REVELATION 7:1-3

> After these things I saw four angels standing on the four corners of the earth, holding the four winds of the earth, that the wind should not blow on the earth, nor on the sea, nor on any tree (Rev. 7:1).

It is interesting that these angels are holding back the winds from blowing. How long could you survive in the Los Angeles basin if we didn't have the winds carrying the smog elsewhere? Just a few still days with slight winds and we practically asphyxiate. Here the angels are holding the winds and halting the wind movement upon the earth for a period of time.

> And I saw another angel ascending from the east, having the seal of the living God: and he cried with a loud voice to the four angels, to whom it was given to hurt the earth and the sea, saying, Hurt not the earth, neither the sea, nor the trees, till we have sealed the servants of our God in their foreheads (Rev. 7:2–3).

In Revelation 8 there are the seven trumpet judgments. John sees seven angels; each has a trumpet. As they sound their trumpets, judgments take place upon the earth. The four angels John sees standing in the four corners of the earth are possibly the first four of the seven angels that bring the seven trumpet judgments.

There are some people who try to "put down" the Bible because of this particular verse: "standing at the four corners of the earth." They say, "The Bible can't be inspired by God because these writers are reflecting the scientific mind of their age, thinking that the world was flat. John could not be writing by inspiration of God, for he never would have said 'the four corners of the earth.' We know that the earth is round." However, in Isaiah 40:22, the Bible refers to the earth as being a "circle," not as being flat.

A few years ago the United States Marines Corps was bragging that our Marines are "in the four corners of the world." Does that mean the United States government believes the flat earth theory? Don't they know that the earth is round? John wasn't talking about a flat earth. We have the north, east, south, and west. "Four corners of the earth" is a figure of speech which is still used today.

These four angels are ready to bring forth their judgments upon the earth, but a fifth angel comes on the scene to halt the action and seal the servants of God in their foreheads. This seal is actually God writing His name in their foreheads.

REVELATION 7:4-8

"I heard the number of them which were sealed: and there were sealed an hundred and forty four thousand of all the tribes of the children of Israel" (Rev. 7:4). It is sad that so many groups are trying to identify themselves as the 144,000.

Let me first say that I don't want to be one of them, even if I were a Jew of Israel. I wouldn't want to be around during the tribulation period. Thus, I have no desire to identify with the 144,000. But groups come along all the time trying to make themselves this exclusive group.

The Jehovah's Witnesses identify themselves as the 144,000. They claimed they were the only ones who would get into heaven. Then in the 1930s they reached their 144,000 faithful witnesses. They had to do something else because the Lord didn't come when they thought He would. Thus, they've made a new multitude which will dwell upon the earth. These won't make the heavenly scene but will live in peace upon the earth and bear children in the kingdom age. That's the chief goal of the Jehovah's Witnesses today, because they say that heaven is full.

The late Herbert W. Armstrong of the *World Tomorrow Program* declared that his organization is the 144,000. Once they get their hooks into you and you faithfully start to support their program, they'll send you a mailing when the time is come to flee to the wilderness. They have prepared a place where you might survive the last part of the great tribulation.

But let's look at these things without twisting the Scriptures by trying to spiritualize them.

Some say that "Israel" in Revelation 7:4 is spiritual Israel. If Israel is spiritual, why isn't the number "144,000" also spiritual? Maybe that's a spiritual number. Maybe that's symbolic of 144 million. Maybe the Jehovah's Witnesses can take a few more into heaven. They say that one part of Revelation 7:4 is spiritual and the other part is literal. Why would God mix the literal with the spiritual? So that you couldn't really understand?

I believe in reading the Bible as it is. I was talking with a Jehovah's Witness one day regarding the 144,000. "Now, just a minute," I said. "The only way you could have gotten that weird idea is to listen to some false teacher. You never could have gotten it by just reading the Bible!"

He answered, "But it really doesn't mean *that*. You see, *that* means *this*." In other words, God didn't mean what He said.

But read what it says: "There were sealed 144,000 of all the tribes of the children of Israel." That doesn't sound very confusing. It sounds very plain to me. The 144,000 are of all the tribes of the children of Israel. I find no difficulty in understanding that at all. Any other interpretation would have to twist the meaning. You'd have to read something into it.

A lot of unnecessary confusion has been created by attempting to spiritualize the text. Those who seek to identify themselves as the 144,000 refuse to see that God will still deal with the nation

Israel. They refuse to see the seventieth "seven" of Daniel (Daniel 9:24–27). They refuse to see the place of Israel in prophecy. This so totally messes up the whole concept of prophecy that nothing makes sense.

This is what the Word says: God is dealing with the nation Israel during this last seven-year period known as the great tribulation. It is the seventieth "seven" prophesied by Daniel. It is also known as "the time of Jacob's trouble" (Jeremiah 30:7).

God has in times past sealed the nation Israel against plagues. In Exodus God said,

> This night I will pass through the land and I will slay the firstborn in every house. In order that your firstborn might be spared, take a lamb and slay it and put its blood on the lintel and the doorposts of your houses. When I pass through the land and I see the blood on the door, I will pass over the house, and the firstborn will not be slain within that house (Exodus 12:3–14).

God had the children of Israel put a special seal upon their houses which actually separated them from the Egyptians. When the Lord passed through the land that night, all the firstborn of all the families were slain except those in the houses protected by the blood on the doorpost.

Ezekiel 9 speaks of the judgment that was to come upon the people. Again, there was a halt in the action, for, before judgment came, an angel with an inkhorn was told to mark those who were crying out because of the abominations taking place in the land. When the judgment came, those marked by the angel would be spared.

This is probably the same situation that we find in Revelation 7:4—a special group is marked.

There is confusion only because some people say, "God didn't say what He meant. Let me tell you what God meant to say." The Jehovah's Witnesses will tell you what God meant to say, the Mormons will tell you what God meant to say. "They all say different things, so who am I to believe?" God's Word is not confusing, just man's attempt to interpret it.

It was almost as though God anticipated this kind of jugglery with His Word and so He became very specific. God didn't just say "Israel" when introducing the 144,000 He went further and listed the twelve tribes.

Paul said we are the children of Abraham by faith (Galatians 3:7). Abraham was the father of those who believed. Yet, the Scripture never tries to make spiritual tribes. There is a spiritual Israel, the church, but they seem to be divided into denominations, not tribes. When you start getting back to tribes then you're back to the physical descendants of Abraham. The tribes of the children of Israel are from the physical seed of Abraham, not the spiritual seed.

So, just in case people would try to spiritualize this group and confuse the prophetic understanding, the Lord named the twelve tribes from which each twelve thousand would come to be sealed.

"Of the tribe of Judah were sealed twelve thousand; of the tribe of Reuben, twelve thousand." And twelve thousand were also sealed from each of the following tribes: Gad, Asher, Naphtali, Manasseh, Simeon, Levi, Issachar, Zebulun, Joseph, and Benjamin (Rev. 7:58).

It is interesting that twelve tribes are always listed in the Bible (twelve is the number of government). In reality, we find some tribes listed here that are not mentioned in other listings. As a general rule, Levi is never listed as one of the twelve tribes.

Actually, two tribes were added to the children of Israel. There were twelve sons of Jacob, but then Jacob adopted the two sons of Joseph, Jacob's grandsons Ephraim and Manasseh. These also became tribes of Israel. In the Old Testament most of the listings omit Levi and Joseph and, instead, have Ephraim and Manasseh added to these lists. But here in Revelation 7 Dan and Ephraim are omitted and Levi and Joseph are inserted.

Why is it that Dan and Ephraim are not sealed and the tribe of Levi and Joseph are listed instead? In Deuteronomy God said that if any person, kindred, family, or tribe shall lead the children of Israel into idolatry, then they shall be cut off from among the nations (Deuteronomy 29:18–21). Dan and Ephraim were the two tribes in which the two golden calves were built as idols in the northern kingdom by Jeroboam. These tribes were cut off according to God's Word. Thus, they are not sealed and protected.

This means that Dan and Ephraim will have to go through and suffer the full ravages of the great tribulation. The others are sealed so that the winds do not hurt them. In Revelation 9 the demons that come out of the *abyss* are told not to hurt those who have the seal of God in their foreheads, referring to the 144,000. Twelve thousand from each tribe are spared much of the judgment of God.

Though Dan and Ephraim are not listed in Revelation (see 1 Kings 12:28–31), when the Lord comes and establishes His kingdom and again reapportions the land according to Ezekiel, the very first portion goes to the tribe of Dan (Ezekiel 48:1). Even though Dan was led into idolatry and was not sealed, Dan is the first one to get his portion. So many times we have failed in God's purposes, yet God in His loving grace restores and gives again. Blessed be the name of the LORD!

REVELATION 7:9-17

After this I beheld, and, lo, there was a great multitude, which no man could number, of all of the nations, and kindreds, and people, and tongues, and they stood before the throne, and before the Lamb, clothed with white robes, and palms in their hands (Rev. 7:9).

This is a great multitude of people—a numberless multitude. These, I believe, are the same that we saw "under the altar" in the fifth seal in Revelation 6, clothed with white robes, crying, "O Lord, how long until You avenge our blood?" They were told to wait. But now the total number that were to be slain as those in

Revelation 6 were slain has been fulfilled. They now take their place in the heavenly scene. Out of all the nations, people, and tongues, they stand clothed with white robes and palms in their hands before the throne and before the Lamb.

I do not believe that this "great multitude" is the church. First of all, the elder said unto John, "Who are these, and where did they come from?" (Rev. 7:13). The very nature of the question implies that they were a group of people in heaven whom John didn't recognize.

John answered, "You know." If they were the Old Testament saints, John would have known them, even as Peter, James and John knew Moses and Elijah on the Mount of Transfiguration. If this group were the church, John would have certainly recognized them because he had no difficulty recognizing the church in heaven. John knew the mystery of the church by this time—that God was going to gather out of the Gentile nations the body of Christ. This had been revealed to the apostle Paul and through him to the church. John was on Patmos at the time of the revelation, but he had been ministering in one of the Gentile churches in Ephesus. He knew all about the church.

But John doesn't know this great multitude out of all the nations which no man can number. And so the elder answers him and tells him who they are. "These are they who came out of the great tribulation, and have washed their robes, and made them white in the blood of the Lamb" (Rev. 7:14).

They are those who have been martyred during the tribulation period—those who have refused to take the mark of the beast and refused to bow to the Antichrist or to his image, and who kept their testimony and the faith of Jesus Christ.

Notice that, though this "great multitude" is brought into the heavenly scene, they aren't brought into the same position as the church. "Therefore are they before the throne of God, and serve him day and night in his temple: and He who sits on the throne shall dwell among them" (Rev. 7:15). They're before the throne of God serving Him day and night.

The church, on the other hand, is not in heaven as a servant. The church is there as the Bride of Christ, married to Him. We shall live and reign with Jesus Christ.

This great multitude is crying with a loud voice saying,

> Salvation to our God who sits upon the throne, and unto the Lamb. And all the angels stood round about the throne, and about the elders and the four living creatures, and fell before the throne on their faces, and worshiped God (Rev. 7:1–11).

This worship took place previously in Revelation 4—the first of the heavenly scenes that John saw. When the cherubim worshiped God, the twenty-four elders fell on their faces and cast their crowns before the throne of God.

As this great multitude is declaring glory unto God and worshiping and praising God and Jesus Christ for the salvation they have received, the living creatures (the cherubim) and the twenty-four elders fall on their faces before the throne and worship God. "Saying, Amen: Blessing, and glory, and wisdom, and thanksgiving, and honor, and power, and might, be unto our God for ever and ever. Amen" (Rev. 7:12).

Notice that their worship of God ascribes to Him blessings, glory, wisdom, thanksgiving, honor, power and might.

Having gone through a great portion of the tribulation—through the time of famine and polluted waters—they have experienced tremendous hunger and thirst. But "they shall hunger no more, neither thirst any more; neither shall the sun light on them, nor any heat" (Rev. 7:16). (In Revelation 16, God gives the sun power to scorch men who dwell upon the earth.)

> For the Lamb which is in the midst of the throne shall shepherd them, and shall lead them unto living fountains of waters: and God shall wipe away all tears from their eyes (Rev. 7:17).

CHAPTER 8

CALAMITIES

We've gone through six seals and now we come to the seventh seal. Out of the seventh seal we find the seven trumpets of judgments, and out of the trumpet judgments we find the seven vials of God's wrath. All this is contained in the seventh seal.

REVELATION 8:1-2

When he had opened the seventh seal, there was silence in heaven about the space of half an hour (Rev. 8:1).

What is the significance of the silence? We really don't know. It's interesting that explanations and commentaries have been written about this silence in heaven for the space of a half an hour. Man can't seem to be quiet about silence in heaven. But where the Bible is silent, it's best that we keep silent, too. Silence—that awe before this trumpet judgment of God comes forth.

"And I saw the seven angels which stood before God; and to them were given seven trumpets" (Rev. 8:2). Some say that these "angels" are seven archangels.

Only one angel in the Scripture is referred to as an archangel—Michael (Jude 9). He's one of the leading angels. Gabriel called Michael "one of the chief princes" (Daniel 10:13).

Gabriel is another angel that stands in the presence of God. He came to Zacharias as he was ministering in the temple and announced that his wife Elizabeth was to bear a child in her old age. Gabriel told Zacharias to call his name John. Zacharias said, "How can I know this? For I am an old man, and my wife well stricken in years." The angel answered, "I am Gabriel, that stands in the presence of God; and am sent to... show you these glad tidings" (Luke 1:18–19). The angels Gabriel and Michael stand in the presence of God.

In the book of Enoch, one of the books of the Apocrypha, there are listed the names of six angels: Raphael, Michael, Gabriel, Uriel, Raquel, and Sarakiel. The book of Enoch calls them holy angels. Whether they all stand in the presence of God we don't know; we do know that Gabriel and Michael are two of the angels standing in His presence.

REVELATION 8:3-6

> And another angel came and stood at the altar, having a golden censer; and there was given unto him much incense, that he should offer it with the prayers of all saints upon the golden altar which was before the throne. And the smoke of the incense, which came with the prayers of the saints, ascended up before God out of the angel's hand. And the angel took the censer, and filled it with fire of the altar, and cast it into the earth: and there were voices, and thunderings, and lightnings, and an earthquake. And the seven angels which had the seven trumpets prepared themselves to sound (Rev. 8:3–6).

Here we see the heavenly scene. We see again the golden censers with incense mingled with the prayers of the saints.

The people of biblical times were very familiar with the imagery in the book of Revelation. It is rather foreign to us. In the Old Testament the golden censer was used by the priest who daily went into the tabernacle. He'd take some coals off the altar, place them in this little golden censer, and add some incense to it. As the smoke of the incense rose, he'd enter the tabernacle and wave this golden censer before the altar. The smoke of the incense rising would be as the sweetness of the prayers of God's people. The priest would thus intone his prayers to God for the nation Israel.

It's important to realize that the actions of the priest, combined with the whole earthly tabernacle, were a model or a pattern of the heavenly things. Here in Revelation 8:2–6 we see the heavenly scene of which the earthly tabernacle was a model. We see the angel taking the coals from the altar and mingling it with the incense, the prayers of the saints.

REVELATION 8:7-11

> The first angel sounded, and there followed hail and fire mingled with blood, and they were cast upon the earth: and the third part of the trees was burned up, and all green grass was burned up (Rev. 8:7).

The first of the trumpet judgments affects the earth and the vegetation upon the earth. If we're having difficulty feeding the people now, what will happen when one-third of the food supplies are wiped out by this trumpet judgment? The grass will be wiped out and one third of all the trees. Hail and fire mingled with blood will be cast to the earth, and the trees and the green grass will be burned.

> The second angel sounded, and as it were a great mountain burning with fire was cast into the sea: and the third part of the sea became blood; and the third part of the creatures which were in the sea, and had life, died; and the third part of the ships were destroyed (Rev. 8:8–9).

This great mountain of fire falling into the sea sounds like pollution. The earth will be so polluted that the trees will be dying. That is happening now. The strontium 90 from a nuclear fallout in the atmosphere affects vegetation and greatly endangers our lives. That's why the atmospheric testing of nuclear weapons was stopped. If a nuclear war breaks out, the by-product of radioactive fallout will do tremendous damage to crops and the earth. It would become possible that the sea will become polluted, and the third part of the creatures die, and the third part of the ships be destroyed.

> The third angel sounded, and there fell a great star from heaven, burning as it were a lamp, and it fell upon the third part of the rivers, and upon the fountains of waters; and the name of the star is called Wormwood... and many men died of the waters, because they were made bitter (Rev. 8:10–11).

The third trumpet judgment affects the fresh water supply. One-third of the rivers and the fresh water supplies of the earth are destroyed. Imagine the thirst that will ensue when one-third of the fresh water supplies are destroyed. Already the environmentalist are rightly concerned about the pollution of our fresh water supplies that endanger mankind.

REVELATION 8:12-13

> The fourth angel sounded, and the third part of the sun was smitten, and the third part of the moon, and the third part of the stars; so as the third part of them was darkened, and the day shone not for a third part of it, and the night likewise. And I beheld, and heard an angel flying through the midst of heaven, saying with a loud voice, Woe, woe, woe, to the inhabiters of the earth by reason of the other voices of the trumpet of the three angels, which are yet to sound! (Rev. 8:12–13).

The first four angels have sounded, but then another angel came flying through the midst of the heavens, declaring with a loud voice, "Woe, woe, woe." These signs in the heaven are the fulfillment of the Scripture (Matthew 24:29).

The fourth angel darkens the sun and the moon so that they only shine for a third part. It is probably an atmospheric condition created as a result of these first three trumpets.

We do know that when Krakatoa, the volcanic island in the South Pacific, erupted it just blew itself apart. The oceans went rushing into this crater as it exploded. It was a mighty convulsion. In fact, the explosion was heard two thousand miles away. The island was obliterated—it just disappeared. Sunsets around the world were colored by dust for two years as a result of that tremendous explosion in which at least one cubic mile of material was blown into the air.

In a recent winter we had extremely beautiful sunsets that resulted from the volcanoes erupting in Guatemala. These volcanoes gave us some very colorful sunsets because of the ash and suspended dust material that filled the atmosphere.

These plagues striking the earth, sea, and fresh water appear to have the effect within the atmosphere of darkening the sun and the moon and causing the moon to take on the appearance of blood.

CHAPTER 9

MISERY, WOE, AND SUFFERING

REVELATION 9:1

The Abyss—

And the fifth angel sounded, and I saw a star fall from heaven [a fallen star] unto the earth; and to him was given the key of the bottomless pit [*abyss*] (Rev. 9:1).

The *abyss* is literally a shaft.

Somewhere upon the surface of the earth there is a shaft. The entrance to this shaft leads down into the heart of the earth where Hades exists. Hades is often translated "hell" in the Bible. Hell does exist. It's in the center of the earth.

When the Pharisees came to Jesus and asked Him for a sign, He said,

An evil and adulterous generation seeks after a sign; but no sign will be given it, except the sign of the prophet Jonah; for as Jonah was three days and three nights in the whale's belly; so shall the Son of man be three days and three nights in the heart of the earth (Matthew 24:29).

Paul tells us,

He who has ascended is the same one who first of all descended into the lower parts of the earth. When he ascended up on high, he led captivity captive, and gave gifts unto men (Ephesians 4:8–10).

When anyone from the Old Testament died, they went to Hades. That is why in the Old Testament Hades is referred to as the "grave" and "hell." It was the abiding place of everyone who died, but it was divided into two sections.

Jesus told us about this division when He talked about the rich man and Lazarus (Luke 16:19–31). A certain rich man fared sumptuously every day. A beggar was brought, daily covered with sores. The poor man died and was carried by the angels into Abraham's bosom. Also, the rich man died and went into Hades. He lifted up his eyes being in torment and, seeing Abraham afar off, and Lazarus being comforted, he cried unto him and said, "Father Abraham, have mercy upon me, and send Lazarus, that he may dip the tip of his finger in water, and cool my tongue; for I am tormented in this flame."

Abraham said,

Son, remember that you in your lifetime received the good things, and likewise Lazarus evil things: but now he is comforted, and you are tormented. And besides all this, between us and you there is a great gulf fixed: so that they which would pass from here to you cannot; neither can they pass to us, that would come from there.

"Then I pray you," the rich man said "that you would send him to my father's house for I have five brethren; that he may testify unto them, lest they also come into this place of torment."

This man was not sleeping. He was very conscious in Hades. Lazarus also was conscious. He was being comforted in Abraham's bosom.

In another biblical allusion to Hades, Jesus said to the thief on the cross, "Today you will be with me in paradise" (Luke 23:43). And they descended into Hades.

In the second chapter of Acts, Peter on the day of Pentecost stood up to preach. A crowd had gathered to observe the interesting phenomena of the sound of a mighty rushing wind and they heard people magnifying God in many languages. When they questioned what this meant, Peter told them, "This is that which was spoken by the prophet Joel." Then Peter began his sermon by declaring,

Men of Israel, hear these words; Jesus of Nazareth, a man approved of God among you by miracles and wonders and signs, which God did by him in the midst of you, as you yourselves also know: him, being delivered by the determinate counsel and foreknowledge of God, you have taken, and by wicked hands have crucified and slain; whom God has raised up, having loosed the pains of death: because it was not possible that he should be held by it.

And then Peter quoted from one of the prophetic Messianic psalms of David. "David speaks concerning him... You will not leave my soul in hell, neither will You suffer Your Holy One to see corruption. And so," Peter said,

I testify unto you that God did not leave His soul in Hades. But this same Jesus has God raised from the dead and He is ascended at the right hand of the Father, and He has now shed abroad this which you see (Acts 2:14–36).

When Jesus died He descended into Hades and preached, according to Peter, to those souls in prison (1 Peter 3:19). According to Paul, when Jesus ascended He led these captives from their captivity (Ephesians 4:8). He emptied that portion of Hades where the faithful with Abraham had waited for God to fulfill His promises. Speaking of Abraham and all these people of faith in the Old Testament period, the Bible says, "For these all died in faith, not having received the promise: God having provided some better thing for us, that they without us should not be made complete" (Hebrews 11:39–40). They could not come into the heavenly scene until the blood of Jesus Christ had been shed for the sins of the world. The Old Testament sacrifice had covered their sin. Their faith that God would send the Messiah brought them salvation. God imputed their faith in Christ for righteousness. But they couldn't be brought into the heavenly scene until Jesus descended and led them out of prison.

Isaiah speaks of Christ's ministry of opening the prison to those that are bound (Isaiah 61:1). Jesus was to open the prison to those that were bound by death. It was not possible, the Scripture

said, that He could be held by death (Romans 6:9). So, he broke
the bars of the prison of death and led captivity captive when He
ascended on high.

The *abyss* is the place of incarceration for demons or evil
spirits. The demons who possessed the man of Gadarenes said to
Jesus, "Do not send us to the *abyss* before our time" (Luke
8:26–31). They pleaded with Him that they might still have liberty
on the earth. They realize the time is coming when they'll be
consigned to the *abyss* for a thousand years during the millennial
reign of Christ.

The Bible tells us that the Antichrist will ascend out of the
abyss. "The beast that you saw was, and is not; and shall ascend out
of the *abyss*" (Rev. 17:8). The beast was already upon the earth at
one time. He is coming back to the earth, ascending out of the
abyss where he has been incarcerated.

The Bible then tells us that Satan will be bound with a great
chain and cast into the *abyss* at the return of Jesus Christ to the
earth (Rev. 20:1–3).

REVELATION 9:2-4

The Locusts—In the sounding of the fifth trumpet, John sees
the fallen star. A "star" is an angel. The fallen star would no doubt
be Satan. The fallen star is given the key to this *abyss*. As he
opened the pit of the *abyss*, "there arose a smoke out of the pit, as
the smoke of a great furnace; and the sun and the air were
darkened by reason of the smoke of the pit" (Rev. 9:2). The pit,
more or less, is as a great volcano belching smoke and darkening
the sun and polluting the air around the earth.

> And there came out of the smoke locusts [or locust-like
> creatures] upon the earth: and unto them was given power,
> as the scorpions of the earth have power. And it was
> commanded them that they should not hurt the grass of
> the earth, neither any green thing, neither any tree; but
> only those men which have not the seal of God in their
> foreheads (Rev. 9:34).

This is another mention of the 144,000. They were previously sealed so that they would not be hurt by the angels holding the four winds, ready to bring the suffering upon the earth (Rev. 7:3). Now the 144,000 are spared the pain to be inflicted by these demons turned loose upon the earth. These demons have the appearance of locusts.

There's a very interesting book called *Through Forbidden Tibet* by Harrison Forman. He has a chapter called, "I Saw the King of Hell." He talks about an annual religious rite in Tibet where the religious men of the nation gather and call forth various demons—the demon of famine, the demon of floods, etc.—and they materialize.

Forman writes that the "priests" exercise their spiritual powers over these demons so that the demons cannot affect the land in the coming year. But a demon may happen to get away. For instance, if the demon of floods escapes, then the land is ravished by floods in the coming year. At the conclusion of this week-long ceremony, they call forth the King of Hell. Forman describes how he sought to guard himself against falling into any hypnotic state or trance and kept doing things to protect himself against becoming hypnotized. What he saw was uncanny. He actually saw demons as they materialized, and he describes them and their various forms. His descriptions of the demons are much like those in Revelation.

Satan, the fallen star, the fallen angel, opens this shaft and from it comes the smoke, and out of the smoke come demons who go forth upon the earth. Their power is as a scorpion—the power to inflict pain upon those who dwell upon the earth.

The 144,000 are protected from these demonic creatures. This shows that the locusts have intelligence; they're able to discern the 144,000 that have the seal of God upon their foreheads. God is again protecting His own from Satan's attacks.

REVELATION 9:5-6

To them it was given that they should not kill them, but that they should be tormented for five months: and their torment was as the torment of a scorpion, when it strikes a man. And in those days shall men seek death, and shall not find it; and shall desire to die, and death shall flee from them (Rev. 9:5–6).

Death is almost personified in the Scripture. Paul cried, "O death, where is your sting?" In literature, death is spoken of as grasping hold of people. "He's caught in the grasp of death." In Revelation 20 death and hell will be cast into the lake of fire (v. 14). Death and hell will give up their dead to stand before God. Death will release its grasp, hell will release its grip, and men will stand before the judgment throne of God.

For five months death takes a holiday. I can't think of anything more horrible than not being able to die when the time to die has come.

A woman called one night where I was ministering and said, "Chuck, come over quick. I'm in trouble."

I said, "What's the matter?"

She said, "I think my son has killed himself. I'm afraid to take a look because he might shoot me. I want you to go and see." Then she said, "He likes you." Her son was having a problem with alcohol and I had been counseling him.

He had come home drunk. His mother said, "Oh, son, how long are you going to break your mother's heart over your drinking?"

He said, "You won't have to worry about me anymore." He went into his room and she heard a shot. She was afraid to do anything.

I went back into the room and I saw him lying on the floor. He had put a .45 to his right temple and had blown out the whole side of his head. I picked pieces of skull and hair off the ceiling. They were embedded in the plaster. It was one of the goriest sights I had ever seen. After they had taken away his body, they didn't clean up. I had to scrape up his brains with a dust pan and flush them down the toilet.

I didn't sleep for about a week. It was a very terrifying experience. Yet I thought, what if death would not come? What if you would do something like that to your body but still couldn't die? You'd be walking around in that condition and you'd just continue to live. Death really is a blessing at many times. Death isn't the worst thing that can happen to you.

There is coming a time of great torment. Demons will be going around inflicting pain like scorpions. People will be seeking to die, actually attempting to commit suicide, but their spirits will not leave their bodies, and they'll go on in their mangled frames.

REVELATION 9:7-12

> And the shapes of the locusts were like horses that were prepared to battle; and on their heads were crowns like gold, and their faces were as the faces of men. And they had hair as the hair of women, and their teeth were as the teeth of lions. And they had breastplates, as it were breastplates of iron; and the sound of their wings was as the sound of chariots of many horses running to battle. And they had tails like unto scorpions, and there were stings in their tails: and their power was to hurt men for five months. And they had a king over them, which is the angel of the *abyss* [Satan], whose name in the Hebrew tongue is Abaddon, but in the Greek tongue has his name Apollyon (Rev. 9:7–11).

Both of these names mean "destroyer." Satan is a destroyer. He is the king over these demons.

"One woe is past; and, behold, there come two woes after these things" (Rev. 9:12). Sometimes a person thinks, "If I should miss the rapture, I'll take off for the High Sierras. I'll find a little stream where I can fish and hunt and eat wild berries. I'll hide away so I won't be under the control of the Antichrist. They won't be able to catch me and put the seal on me." Likewise, some people imagine an escape from the judgments of God that are to come upon the earth.

Though you may be able to escape from the Antichrist and his rule, how in the world will you escape from demons? There's no way any person on earth can escape this judgment of God. Don't dream up a scheme or an escape. It won't work.

There's one escape that God has provided. That's in Jesus Christ. Thank God for that escape. We "shall be caught up... to meet the Lord in the air: and so shall we ever be with the Lord" (1 Thessalonians 4:17). I like that! The book of Hebrews asks, "How shall we escape if we neglect so great a salvation?" The truth is, there is no other escape.

REVELATION 9:13-15

"The sixth angel sounded, and I heard a voice from the four horns of the golden altar which is before God" (Rev. 9:13). In the earthly tabernacle there was the altar with four horns upon it. This was a likeness of the heavenly altar, the golden altar which is before God's throne.

The voice John heard was "saying to the sixth angel which had the trumpet, Loose the four angels which are bound at the great river Euphrates" (Rev. 9:14).

The River Euphrates is the river that ran through the ancient Babylonian kingdom from where the world's false religious systems have come. Most of the satanic cults have their origin in Babylon.

The River Euphrates was one of the rivers in the Garden of Eden. The first dwelling place of man was probably in the Euphrates valley. This river is where the four fierce and terrible angels were bound, else they would bring destruction upon the earth.

There are some very interesting verses of Scripture concerning the angels which kept not their first estate (Jude 6; 2 Peter 2:4). They are reserved in chains of darkness, awaiting the day of judgment. It could very well be that those angels are so fierce and horrible that, for the protection of man, God has kept them in chains until this day of judgment. But now God looses them, and they go forth upon the earth wreaking havoc and death upon men.

In the Old Testament, when God was fighting for His people, the Assyrians under King Sennacherib were encamped against the Israelites. God sent an angel of the Lord through the camp of the Assyrians and in one night this angel destroyed 186,000 of the Assyrian army (Isaiah 37:36).

Here in Revelation 9 there are four extremely fierce angels. God has been protecting the earth from them. They have been in chains, but now they are set loose.

"And the four angels were loosed, which were prepared for an hour, and a day, and a month, and a year, to slay a third part of men" (Rev. 9:15). In one hour these angels go forth and wipe out one-third of the earth's population.

If one-fourth of the world's 6.5 billion population is wiped out during the second through the fourth seals, four billion, eight hundred and seventy-five million (4,875,000,000) people would be left upon the earth. Now, one-third (or 1,625,000,000 people) are wiped out during this sixth trumpet judgment. In addition, there are all those destroyed by these other cataclysms—the tidal waves, the earthquake, the meteorite showers, etc. You can see how the earth's population is to be decimated. At this point, only one out of two are surviving, but there's a hint in the Old Testament that only one out of three shall survive (Zechariah 13:9).

REVELATION 9:16-21

The number of the army of the horsemen were two hundred thousand thousand [two hundred million]: and, [John said], I heard the number of them. And thus I saw the horses in the vision, and them that sat on them, having breastplates of fire, and jacinth, and brimstone: and the heads of the horses were as the heads of lions; and out of their mouths issued fire and smoke and brimstone. By these three was the third part of men killed, by the fire, and by the smoke, and by the brimstone, which issued out of their mouths. For their power is in their mouth, and in their tails: for their tails were like unto serpents, and had heads, and with them they do hurt (Rev. 9:16–19).

We are speaking here of a huge army of two hundred million. Do you realize how impossible this was until recent times? How could any nation or combination of nations in the world field an army of two hundred million people? It was only in 1860 that the earth reached a population of one billion Even if every available man alive at the time of John's writing had been mustered, they couldn't have fielded an army of two hundred million.

In 1965 China boasts that she's able to put an army of two hundred million on the field. Isn't that an interesting figure? Why didn't China say 150 million or 175 million or 201 million? Time magazine reported that China declares that she can field an army of two hundred million.[1] And John sees this great army.

Who Is Your God?—

And the rest of the men who were not killed by these plagues yet repented not of the works of their hands, that they should not worship devils (Rev. 9:20).

The most unlikely thing in the world to me and the hardest thing for me to conceive is that a person would consciously worship Satan. I cannot conceive of a mind that would consciously worship the devil. But such is the case. People today are consciously worshiping the devil. In fact, satanic worship is growing.

These people would not repent of their worship of the devil "and their idols of gold, and silver, and brass, and stone, and of wood: which neither can see, nor hear, nor walk" (Rev. 9:20).

We're reminded by David in the Psalms that the idols of the heathen are vain. He said that they carve them out of wood or of silver. Eyes they have but they cannot see. Ears they have but they cannot hear. Feet they have but they cannot walk. Mouths they have but they cannot speak. Those who make them have become altogether like the idols that they have made" (Psalm 135:15–18).

---

[1].   *Time,* May 21, 1965.

Man becomes like his god—that's a basic philosophy of life. Who is your god? You're becoming like your god. Man creates a dumb idol and then himself becomes dumb as he worships it. If your god is false, you're becoming false. If you're worshiping idols, insensate gods, you're becoming insensate. If you're worshiping the true and living God, you're becoming like your God. It can be the greatest curse or the greatest blessing. It all depends on who your god is.

What a blessing to become like our God!

Beloved, now are we the sons of God, and it has not yet appear what we shall be: but we know that, when He shall appear, we shall be like Him [like our God]; for we shall see Him as He is (1 John 3:2).

But we all, with open face beholding... the glory of the Lord, are changed into the same image from glory to glory, even as by the Spirit of the Lord (2 Corinthians 3:18).

What is the master passion of your life? What ideal, philosophy, or ambition controls you? Realize that you're becoming just like your god!

"Neither repented they of their murders, nor of their sorceries" (Rev. 9:21). The word *sorceries* in the Greek is *"pharmakeia,"* from which we get our word "pharmacy." It is the use of drugs for hallucinogenic purposes.

They didn't repent of their sorceries, "nor of their fornication, nor of their thefts" (Rev. 9:21).

You'd think at this point, as the wrath and judgment of God are being poured forth and people are being wiped out all around, that men would be on their knees saying, "O God, have mercy on me a sinner!" But we see the hardness of man's heart; after all this judgment there is no repentance.

Sometimes we say, "Really lay it on him, God, so he'll repent!" But the Scripture says that the goodness of God leads a man to repentance (Romans 2:4). Realizing how good God is amazes me more than anything else. Realizing that I'm so undeserving and knowing the goodness of God brings me to repentance. "O God, how can you be so good to me? I'm such a rotten sinner!" His love leads me to repentance.

CHAPTER 10

FORESHADOWING
OF THE KING

REVELATION 10:1-4

Mighty Angel—

And I saw another mighty angel come down from heaven, clothed with a cloud: and a rainbow was upon his head, and his face was as it were the sun, and his feet as pillars of fire (Rev. 10:1).

By the description I believe this other mighty angel is none other than Jesus Christ. I believe that we have here a picture of the second coming of Jesus Christ.

The word *angel* literally means "messenger." It does not necessarily signify a class of beings. Jesus is coming now as God's Messenger. The very description would almost preclude anyone other than Jesus Christ.

Revelation 1 describes Him: "His countenance [face] was as the sun" and "his feet like unto fine brass, as if they burned in a furnace" (v. 15–16). In Revelation 10:1 Jesus is described as "clothed with a cloud." "Behold, he comes with clouds; and every eye shall see him" (Rev. 1:7). In Matthew 24, Jesus said, "Then they shall see the Son of man coming in the clouds of heaven with power and great glory" (Matthew 24:30). He is coming from heaven clothed with a cloud and a rainbow about His head. (The rainbow was also about the throne of God in Revelation 4.) The rainbow speaks of God's covenant with man. Jesus said that He makes a new covenant with us through His blood (Hebrews 9 & 10). So, He's coming with the sign of the covenant when He comes back to the earth.

"He had in his hand a little book [that was] open" (Rev. 10:2).
The scroll that had been sealed is now open. Jesus is coming back
with the title deed to the earth in His hand.

> And he set his right foot upon the sea, and his left foot on
> the earth, and cried with a loud voice, as when a lion roars:
> and when he had cried, seven thunders uttered their voices
> (Rev. 10:2–3).

When Jesus comes again to the earth He's going to let out a
shout that will be heard around the world. It'll sound like a roaring
lion. It'll be a shout of triumph and victory.

Isaiah prophesied of the coming of Jesus Christ and spoke of
the shout that Jesus utters at this point. "The LORD shall go forth
as a mighty man, He shall stir up jealousy like a man of war: He
shall cry, yea, roar; He shall prevail against His enemies" (Isaiah
42:13). Jeremiah also speaks of this very same event.

> Prophesy against them all these words, and say unto them,
> The LORD shall roar from on high, and utter His voice
> from His holy habitation; He shall mightily roar upon His
> habitation; He shall give a shout, as they that tread the
> grapes, against all the inhabitants of the earth (Jeremiah
> 25:30).

Hosea speaks also of this same event and tells us: "They shall
walk after the LORD, He shall roar like a lion: when He shall roar,
then the children shall tremble from the west" (Hosea 11:10).
Finally, Joel speaks of the same event (Joel 3:16). This coming of
Christ by roaring as a lion has been confirmed by God in the
mouth of two or three witnesses (and more).

After Jesus Christ roared, seven thunders uttered their voices.
"And when the seven thunders had uttered their voices," John said,
"I was about to write: and I heard a voice from heaven saying unto
me, Seal up those things which the seven thunders uttered, and
write them not" (Rev. 10:4). We don't know what the seven
thunders said. There's no way that you can find out until you get
there. When you hear them you'll know what John was told to seal

up. There's no way that we can conjecture on this, and it would be sheer folly to do so.

Interestingly, this means that the Word of God is not complete. John started to write what the seven thunders uttered and the Lord said, "No. Don't write that. Seal it up." We really don't have the *complete* revelation.

REVELATION 10:5-7

No More Delay—

And the angel which I saw stand on the sea and upon the earth lifted up his hand to heaven, and swore by Him who lives for ever and ever, who created heaven, and the things that therein are, and the earth, and the things that therein are, and the sea, and the things which are therein, that there should be time no longer [literally, "that there should be no longer a delay"] (Rev. 10:5–6).

God has delayed taking over the world for a long time. God is still waiting today. We pray, "Thy kingdom come. Thy will be done in earth, as it is in heaven" (Matthew 6:10). But God has delayed His coming. When the Lord comes He'll declare, "There shall be no more delay."

But in the days of the voice of the seventh angel, when he shall begin to sound, the mystery of God should be finished, as He has declared to His servants the prophets (Rev. 10:7).

God promises that the kingdom age will be fulfilled when the voice of the seventh trumpet sounds. Christ shall begin His kingdom reign upon the earth. Therefore, it's significant that in the seventh trumpet He declares, "The kingdoms of this world are become the kingdoms of our Lord, and of his Christ; and he shall reign for ever and ever" (Rev. 11:15). We see the glorious picture of the coming of Jesus Christ with the title deed of the earth—one foot upon the sea, one foot upon the earth, declaring that there shall be no more delay. In the sounding of the seventh trumpet God's kingdom shall be established.

REVELATION 10:8-11

> The voice which I heard from heaven spoke to me again,
> and said, Go and take the little book which is open in the
> hand of the angel which stands upon the sea and upon the
> earth. And I went unto the angel, and said unto him, Give
> me the little book. And he said unto me, Take it, and eat
> it up; and it shall make your belly bitter, but it shall be in
> your mouth sweet as honey. And I took the little book out
> of the angel's hand, and ate it up; and it was in my mouth
> sweet as honey: and as soon as I had eaten it, my belly was
> bitter. And he said unto me, you must prophesy again
> before many peoples, and nations, and tongues, and kings
> (Rev. 10:8–11).

John went to the mighty angel and asked for the little book He
was holding. The angel said, "Eat it." Talk about absorbing a book!
Eating a book is the reading of it, and the book becomes a part of
you. As you read it, in your mouth it's sweet because the things
that it promises are great; but, when you digest it, those things
which must transpire before the fulfillment of its promises are very
bitter and difficult to consider. John found that it was sweet in his
mouth but, as he digested it, it was very bitter. These are the bitter
tragedies and the sufferings the world must experience in the
opening of the seven seals of Revelation prior to the establishment
of the kingdom of God.

The angel told John that he must prophesy again before many
peoples, nations, tongues, and kings. John has prophesied the final
chapter of God's history of man by writing the book of Revelation.

CHAPTER 11

TWO SPECIAL AGENTS

REVELATION 11:1-2

The Temple—John has been recording for us the events that took place as the Lord Jesus opened the seven seals of the scroll held by Him who sits upon the throne. Out of the seventh seal there came forth seven trumpet judgments.

At the beginning of Revelation 11 we have another parenthetical passage (as in Revelation 7 and 10). That is, we break the sequence of events and look at one aspect of the seven-year tribulation period—God's dispatch of two witnesses to the nation Israel.

John said,

> There was given to me a reed [about ten feet long] like unto a rod: and the angel stood, saying, Rise, and measure the temple of God, and the altar, and them that worship therein. But the court which is without the temple leave out, and measure it not; for it is given unto the Gentiles: and the holy city shall they tread under foot for forty-two months (Rev. 11:1–2).

John was given a ten-foot long reed and ordered to measure the temple.

The Jews will rebuild their temple in Jerusalem. This could happen during the first half of the great tribulation period. When the church is taken out and God again deals with Israel during this last seven-year period, the Antichrist will make a covenant with the nation Israel, but in the midst of the seven-year period he'll break that covenant (Daniel 9:27). I believe that in this covenant the

Antichrist will permit Israel to move ahead and rebuild their temple.

At the present time the Jews are making excavations under what is commonly called the Mosque of Omar. But, as close as can be ascertained, the Dome of the Rock Mosque is located at the place of the court of sacrifice in Herod's temple. This is the place where sacrifices were offered, not the sanctuary itself. Many Jewish scholars are convinced that the actual site of the Holy of Holies of Solomon's and also Herod's Temples was 322 feet north of the Dome of the Rock Mosque at a site known today as the Dome of the Spirits and also the Dome of the Tablets.

Orthodox Jews will not go onto the temple mount area at all, because they don't know exactly where the Holy of Holies was located in the original temple, and they don't want to be guilty of walking over it. If, indeed, the site actually is the Holy of Holies, it would situate the Dome of the Rock Mosque in the place of the outer court of the temple of Solomon. Significantly the Lord said to John, "Don't measure the outer court because it is given over to the Gentiles" (Rev. 11:2).

If the Jews have found the site of the Holy of Holies and choose it for the rebuilding of their temple, they won't have to interfere with the Mosque. The Dome of the Rock Mosque is sacred to the Moslems and a holy war would erupt if the Jews ever tried to destroy it in order to build their temple. Thus, diplomatically, the Jews are very careful not to make any reference about building the temple on the Moslem site.

The Jews were to be dispersed. Jesus spoke of their dispersion (Luke 21:24), Daniel prophesied the dispersion (Daniel 9:20–27), and Moses prophesied the dispersion (Deuteronomy 32:26), as did most of the major prophets of the Old Testament. But then they all prophesied about Israel's gathering together in the last days and returning to the land. Jesus said, "Jerusalem shall be trodden down of the Gentiles, until the times of the Gentiles be fulfilled."

Jerusalem was trodden under the foot of the Gentiles until 1967 when the Jews gained control of Jerusalem again. Revelation

11:2 tells us that the Jews will lose control of Jerusalem once more, this time to the Antichrist for a period of forty-two months. It was necessary that the Jews first gain control of the city of Jerusalem before the forty-two months of control by the Antichrist could be fulfilled.

These developments in Jerusalem give us a picture of how we stand in the prophetic order. We are clearly very close to the end.

REVELATION 11:3-5

Two Witnesses—Now God speaks of His two witnesses. God is never without a witness. During the tribulation period not only will there be these two witnesses especially endowed by God, but in Revelation 14 God will even use angels as His witnesses throughout the world.

These two witnesses exist primarily for the sake of the Jews. They are bearing witness to the Jews that Jesus Christ was indeed the Messiah and that they should now turn to Him and receive Him as their Lord and Savior.

Their witness will not be well received. In fact, people will seek to destroy them. "I will give power unto my two witnesses, and they shall prophesy a thousand two hundred and sixty days, clothed in sackcloth" (Rev. 11:3).

Sackcloth was the garment of the prophets and often worn as a sign of mourning over the condition of the nation. These witnesses will be coming with this sign of mourning over the nation to prophesy for three and a half years (forty-two months or 1260 days). This indicates, as does Daniel, that the biblical years of prophecy are predicated on the Babylonian calendar of 360 days to the year.

God will give power to His two witnesses, and they'll prophesy during this period. "These are the two olive trees, and the two candlesticks standing before the God of the earth" (Rev. 11:4).

Zechariah saw an interesting vision. He saw two olive trees growing beside the candlesticks. The branches of the olive trees extended to the candlesticks. Then he saw the olive oil coming from the trees and into the candlesticks, thus giving them a perpetual supply of oil.

In the temple the priest had to take care of the candlesticks daily. He had to fill them with oil and trim the wicks as part of his daily function as priest. Zechariah envisioned a wonderful answer to this daily task, for the olive oil flowed directly from the tree into the candlestick.

The Lord interrupted the vision to Zechariah and said, "This is the word of the LORD unto Zerubbabel, saying, Not by might, nor by power, but by my spirit, says the LORD (Zechariah 4:1–6). The vision actually reveals the glorious and perpetual supply of power that we, as believers, have through the Spirit of God.

These two witnesses are the two candlesticks. The two olive trees speak of their empowering in a mighty way by the Spirit of God.

We see the results of this empowering: "If any man will hurt them, fire proceeds out of their mouth, and devours their enemies: and if any man will hurt them, he must in this manner be killed" (Rev. 11:5).

When Elijah was ministering upon the earth, King Ahaziah sent a captain of fifty men to bring him back as a prisoner. While Elijah was sitting on the mountain, the captain came and said, "You man of God, come down! I'm going to take you to the king." Elijah replied, "If I be a man of God, then let fire come down from heaven and consume you and your fifty men." Fire came down from heaven and consumed the captain with his fifty men.

The king sent out a second captain with fifty men, and the scene was repeated. A third captain with fifty was sent. But this time the captain fell before Elijah and said, "O man of God, have mercy on me. I'm a family man with a wife and children to support. But I'm under orders of the king to take you captive. Would you mind going with me, please?" Elijah went with him (2 Kings 1:1–15). We note that Elijah had called down fire.

Also, when certain of the Samaritans wouldn't receive Jesus in their cities, James and John said, "Lord, do you want us to call down fire from heaven to consume them?" Jesus called James and John "the sons of thunder." They were ready to send lightning on these Samaritans because of their treatment of Jesus Christ.

Jesus said to them, "You know not what manner of spirit you are of. For the Son of man is not come to destroy men's lives, but to save them" and to win the world through love (Luke 9:54–56). But now that the world has rejected His love, God sends fiery judgment upon the earth.

The age of God's grace has come to its conclusion. God deals in judgment with man during the tribulation period. If any man seeks to hurt these two witnesses, fire comes forth and consumes him.

REVELATION 11:6-7

These have power to shut heaven, that it rain not in the days of their prophecy: and have power over waters to turn them to blood, and to smite the earth with all plagues, as often as they will (Rev. 11:6).

Likewise, Elijah went before King Ahab and pronounced that there would be no rain again until he ordered it. God sent a drought to Israel (1 Kings 17:1). The two witnesses have this same power—it will not rain during the time of their prophecy. This will bring a great drought unto the land. In addition, the two witnesses have the power to turn the remaining waters into blood.

Who Are the Two Witnesses?—The identity of the two prophets has often been a matter of conjecture. Many believe that they will be Moses and Elijah, thus representing the law and the prophets. The fact that the water turns to blood and the earth is smitten with plagues seems to speak of Moses. Who would be a greater witness to the nation of Israel than Moses? He is the one to whom the Jews declared allegiance when Jesus was on the earth. In fact, they claimed to be Moses' disciples (John 9:28). It would be very fitting for God to send Moses, representing the law, as a witness of Jesus Christ—for Moses prophesied of Jesus Christ to Israel (Deuteronomy 18:15).

It is fairly certain that the other witness's identity is Elijah. In Malachi God promised to send Elijah before the great and notable day of the Lord (Malachi 4:5). Although John the Baptist was a type of Elijah, he was not the complete fulfillment of this prophecy.

After Jesus descended from the Mount of Transfiguration, He talked to His disciples about the relationship of John the Baptist to Elijah. He said unto them, "Elijah truly shall first come, and restore all things" (Matthew 17:11). He reiterated Malachi's prophecy that Elijah would come before the day of the Lord.

One of the two witnesses is Elijah. The identity of the other witness is a mystery. It is probably Moses or Enoch or, perhaps, Zerubbabel. God spoke to Zerubbabel concerning the relationship of the olive trees and the two candlesticks. It could even be John the Baptist. However, these identities are just suggestions. You can put your own theory in here if you desire.

"And when they shall have finished their testimony..." (Rev. 11:7). I think this is a very appropriate statement. Until the time they finish their testimony, these men are indestructible. No one can touch them. God's anointing and God's hand are upon their lives.

When the two witnesses finish their testimony, then "the beast that ascended out of the *abyss*..." This is the Antichrist. Revelation 17 describes the beast that "was, and is not; and shall ascend out of the *abyss*, and go into Gehenna" (v. 8). The beast that comes out, the Antichrist, "shall make war against them, and shall overcome them, and kill them" (Rev. 11:7). But he cannot overcome them until the two witnesses have finished their testimony.

God's hand and protection was upon the two witnesses until they had completed God's work and plan for their lives. We also have God's hand of protection upon us until we finish our testimony. Once we've finished, who wants to stay around? It's time to go! I have no desire to sit on the shelf someplace and rust away. I'd rather burn-out for Jesus Christ and get it over with in a hurry. I'm ready to get on to the future glory with Jesus.

When the two witnesses finish their testimony, God has better things for them. The beast that came out of the *abyss* had power over them. He overcame them and they were killed.

REVELATION 11:8-14

And their dead bodies shall lie in the street of the great city, which spiritually is called Sodom and Egypt, where also our Lord was crucified (Rev. 11:8).

This is a terrible indictment against Jerusalem, the city that God loved. God said that His eye would always be upon Jerusalem (2 Chronicles 7:16). Yet, it will become so corrupt that God calls it spiritually Egypt, the flesh, and Sodom.

The bodies of the two prophets will lie in the streets of Jerusalem. The people will not even give them a decent burial but will allow their bodies just to lie in the open for three days.

And they of the people and kindreds and tongues and nations shall see their dead bodies for three days and an half, and shall not allow their dead bodies to be put in graves (Rev. 11:9).

The horrible inhumanity of man!

It is interesting, however, that God said that all those who dwell on the earth shall see their dead bodies.

At the time when John wrote, it was impossible for all the world to see the bodies, unless some artist on the scene quickly drew it and sent runners throughout the nations to show the drawing.

But within our generation this has become a very practical reality. Through television or the internet, people sitting in their homes will see the bodies of these two witnesses lying in the street and the people in Jerusalem spitting on them and seeking to mutilate them. It will be televised throughout the world. This prophecy could not have been fulfilled until recent times.

> And they that dwell upon the earth shall rejoice over them, and make merry, and shall send gifts one to another; because these two prophets tormented them that dwelt on the earth (Rev. 11:10).

Man really doesn't want to hear the truth. These two men from God stood up and told the truth. The world is glad to silence the voices of these two prophets. Thus, their death brings on a great celebration, a kind of Christmas celebration—sending gifts, rejoicing, and making merry.

> And after three days and an half the Spirit of life from God entered into them, and they stood upon their feet; and great fear fell upon them which saw them. And they heard a great voice from heaven saying unto them, Come up here. And they ascended up to heaven in a cloud; and their enemies beheld them (Rev. 11:11–12).

Imagine being a TV cameraman on that assignment. You arrive in Jerusalem and focus your camera on these two bodies. Suddenly, they stand up and begin to ascend into heaven. What a shock!

> And the same hour there was a great earthquake [in Jerusalem], and the tenth part of the city fell, and in the earthquake were slain of men seven thousand: and the remnant were afraid, and gave glory to the God of heaven. The second woe is past; and, behold, the third woe comes quickly (Rev. 11:13–14).

There will be a great earthquake in Jerusalem. Jerusalem now has an extensive building program underway. You can imagine the devastation to take place when a tenth part of that city is destroyed by an earthquake.

REVELATION 11:15

The Seventh Trumpet—Now we come back to the trumpets. The seventh trumpet brings the second coming of Jesus Christ.

There have been attempts to relate this "seventh" trumpet with the "last trump" of 1 Corinthians which heralds the rapture of the church (1 Corinthians 15:52). Such an identification only strains the Scripture, and there is no true scriptural evidence to warrant relating the two.

> The seventh angel sounded; and there were great voices in heaven, saying, The kingdoms of this world are become the kingdoms of our Lord, and of his Christ; and he shall reign for ever and ever (Rev. 11:15).

What a glorious day that will be—the day that all Christians throughout the church age have been waiting for. The Old Testament saints were also looking forward to this day. Concerning Abraham and those of faith, the Bible says,

> These all died in faith, not having received the promises, but having seen them afar off… embraced them, and confessed that they were strangers and pilgrims on the earth (Hebrews 11:13).

They "looked for a city [for a kingdom] which has foundations, whose builder and maker is God" (Hebrews 11:10). They were looking forward to this heavenly kingdom and waiting patiently, as the Scriptures tell us, for that day and the sounding of the seventh trumpet (Hebrews 10:36–37).

There are exciting events within our lives that we anxiously look forward to. For instance, there's the day of your marriage. How time seemed to drag as you were waiting for that hour! But once the hour arrived, it went so quickly! The anticipation for the wedding—the countless details and the hours of preparations—all over in fifteen minutes!

Now we wait for this glorious day when the seventh trumpet shall sound and the great voices in heaven declare, "The kingdoms of the world have become the kingdoms of our Lord, and of his Christ; and he shall reign for ever and ever."

The implication here is that the kingdoms of this world are presently not the kingdoms of our Lord and of His Christ. The implication is correct. Satan is the ruler of this world. Man forfeited his rights over to Satan, and Satan became the ruler of the world through Adam's transgression. But Jesus came to redeem the world back to God by purchasing it with His blood. He shall come some day to claim His purchased possession.

As far as the church is concerned, we have been redeemed, and God has given us the Holy Spirit until the redemption of the purchased possession. We belong to Him. Jesus has given us the seal of His Spirit, the down payment of that full work He will do in us through the ages to come.

REVELATION 11:16-17

The time has come when the pronouncement is made: "The twenty-four elders, which sat before God on their thrones, fell upon their faces, and worshiped God" (Rev. 11:16). These elders, it seems, are always falling on their faces! They're before the throne of God, saying, "We give You thanks, O Lord God Almighty, who is, and was, and is to come; because You have taken Your great power, and has reigned" (Rev. 11:17).

God has always had the power and the authority. He could have established the kingdom of God at any time after Jesus paid the price of redemption; but God has now waited almost two thousand years. Yet, we are told in the Scripture to have patience. Wait, for the farmer is waiting for the complete fruit of harvest (James 5:7). So many times I get impatient with the Lord. I get so frustrated by the problems in the world and the seemingly insoluble situations that exist.

In most cities in the United States the crime rate is at epidemic proportions. We had lunch one day with a girl who was robbed the night before. While she was in the apartment some fellow took vise-grip pliers and twisted off the front door handle. She was dialing the police as he busted the chain and pushed open the door, wrenching off the screws. He stole her television set while she was on the phone with the police. He escaped over the back fence. Fortunately, the TV didn't work.

Living in these days, I get impatient. I say, "O Lord, why have you waited so long? Come quickly!" Yet, when I think of my same prayer five years ago, I'm glad that He waited. During that time so many people have been added to the kingdom. The patience and waiting of the Lord is the salvation of the lost. For God is "not willing that any should perish, but that all should come to repentance" (2 Peter 3:9). God is giving opportunity for men to repent. Thus, the delay is salvation to those who will believe.

But God said to Noah, "My spirit shall not always strive with man" (Genesis 6:3), and we realize that the age of grace is closing out and rapidly coming to an end. God is going to move on with the things of His eternal kingdom.

REVELATION 11:18-19

"The nations were angry, and Your wrath is come" (Rev. 11:18). In Psalms we read, "Why do the heathen rage, and the people imagine a vain thing?" (Psalm 2:1). The nations are angry.

At the first coming of Christ, those who really opposed Him were the rulers of the day. They were all fearful of losing their places. The wise men who followed the star from the East came to Herod and inquired, "Where is he who is born King of the Jews?" (Matthew 2:1–4).

Herod was king of the Jews. He didn't want anyone to supplant him. He told the wise men, "When you have found Him [the Child], bring me word again, that I may come and worship Him also" (Matthew 2:8). But Herod had no intention of worshiping Jesus. He had every intention of destroying Him, because his own position was being threatened.

The rulers of the Jews turned Jesus over to Pilate because they were fearful of losing their position. They said among themselves, "All the people are going after Him! What are we going to do if they all receive Him as their Messiah?" (Mark 11:18; 15:10). Because they were fearful of losing their ruling position, the Jewish leaders crucified Him. Jesus Christ shook the rulers of the world.

At the second coming, the nations will again be angry. The first time Jesus was here they said, "We will not have this man to rule over us." But He's coming to rule with a rod of iron.

> The time of the dead [has come], that they should be judged, and that You should give reward unto Your servants the prophets, and to the saints, and them that fear Your name, small and great; and should destroy them who destroy the earth (Rev. 11:18).

Daniel wrote that the time will come when those in the grave shall be raised. "Many of them that sleep in the dust of the earth shall awake, some to everlasting life, and some to shame and everlasting contempt" (Daniel 12:2). We know from Revelation 20 that there will be the thousand-year period of time known as the Millennium separating the resurrections of the righteous dead from the unrighteous dead.

> And the temple of God was opened in heaven, and there was seen in his temple the ark of his testament: and there were lightnings, and voices, and thunderings, and an earthquake, and great hail (Rev. 11:19).

CHAPTER 12

PEOPLE AND PLACES

REVELATION 12:1-2

In Revelation 12 we are introduced to a variety of personages.

> And there appeared a great wonder in heaven; a woman clothed with the sun, and the moon under her feet, and upon her head a crown of twelve stars. And she being with child cried, travailing in birth, and pained to be delivered (Rev. 12:1–2).

Because of the description, I believe this "woman" in heaven is the nation Israel.

Jacob had twelve sons. Joseph was the eleventh son of Jacob. Because Jacob loved Joseph, his brothers became very jealous of him. Once Joseph had a dream in which he was binding his sheaf of corn and his brothers were binding theirs, but all their sheaves bowed down to his sheaf. When Joseph told them his dream, they became even angrier with him and said, "You think we're going to bow down to you? You've got another thing coming!"

Joseph had another dream which he told his father. "I dreamed that the sun and the moon and the eleven stars bowed down unto me." Jacob rebuked his son Joseph and said, "It's wrong to think that your mother, your brothers, and I will all bow to you." The sun and the moon referred to Jacob and his wife. The eleven stars referred to the eleven brothers (Genesis 37:5–10). This dream was fulfilled when Joseph became the Prime Minister of Egypt and his brothers came to buy grain from him. Therefore, the sun, moon, and eleven stars speak of the nation of Israel.

REVELATION 12:3-4

> And there appeared another wonder in heaven; and behold
> a great red dragon, having seven heads and ten horns, and
> seven crowns upon his heads. And his tail drew the third
> part of the stars of heaven, and did cast them to the earth:
> and the dragon stood before the woman which was ready
> to be delivered, for to devour her child as soon as it was
> born (Rev. 12:3–4).

The second personage of Revelation 12 is this "great red
dragon" with seven heads and ten horns. The dragon, of course, is
Satan. The dragon has always been the symbol for Satan.

In Chinese parades people run underneath a huge paper
concoction. As it twists and turns through the street, it gives you an
allusion of a floating dragon. As part of the curse after Adam and
Eve had sinned, the serpent was to go upon its belly in the dust
(Genesis 3:14). Some of you have lovely dragons in your homes as
artifacts. Personally, I wouldn't want one.

The fact that the dragon draws a third part of the stars with his
tail perhaps indicates that Satan at his fall took with him a third of
the angelic beings. Prior to his rebellion, Satan was in the garden of
God and had every precious stone for his covering. He was perfect
in beauty, perfect in wisdom, perfect in all his ways—until iniquity
was found in him (Ezekiel 28:11–15). Satan had tremendous
influence, yet God cast him forth from heaven and his position and
authority. However, Satan still had access to heaven.

In Job, when the sons of God were presenting themselves unto
God, Satan also came with them. God said unto Satan, "Where
have you been?" He replied, "Going to and fro through the earth."
God said, "Have you considered my servant Job, an upright man,
one who fears God, and loves good and hates evil, a perfect man?"
Satan began to accuse Job before God (Job 1:6-11). Later in
Revelation 12 Satan is called the accuser of the brethren, accusing
them before God day and night continually (v. 10).

Not only does Satan accuse us before God, but he accuses us to
ourselves. He's quick to jump on our weaknesses and our faults,

trying to drive us away from God's grace and mercy. He tries to make us afraid to come to God. He points to our own weaknesses and tells us how unworthy and how undeserving we are. Yet, God is gracious and merciful, and He bestows His love and His grace upon us even though we are unworthy.

There were angels which kept not their first estate (Jude 6). When Jesus faced the demonic Gadarene, He asked him his name. He replied, "Legion, for we are many" (Mark 5:9). There are many evil spirits, demons, fallen angels, principalities, and powers of darkness and evil who align themselves with Satan's rebellion against God's authority.

REVELATION 12:5-6

> And she [the woman] brought forth a man Child, who was to rule all nations with a rod of iron: and her Child was caught up unto God, and to His throne. And the woman fled into the wilderness, where she had a place prepared of God, that they should feed her there for a thousand two hundred and sixty days (Rev. 12:5–6).

The man Child is thought to be Christ, because the verse speaks of Him as the one who is to rule all nations with a rod of iron and He has been caught up to His throne. We know that Jesus is at the right hand of the throne in heaven. And we know that He shall rule all nations with a rod of iron. "Ask of Me," God said,

> and I shall give You the heathen for Your inheritance, and the uttermost parts of the earth for Your possession. You shall break them with a rod of iron; you shall dash them in pieces like a potter's vessel (Psalm 2:8–9).

It is significant that, when addressing the church of Thyatira, Jesus promised to him "who overcomes… will I give power over the nations: and he shall rule them with a rod of iron; as the vessels of a potter shall they be broken to shivers" (Rev. 2:26–27). This is a promise to the church of Thyatira to rule over the nations and to sit in their thrones in the kingdom of God. Therefore, sitting upon the throne and ruling over the nations with a rod of iron is not an exclusive ministry of Jesus Christ, but also belongs to the overcomers. This has caused some to identify the woman as the church and the man Child as elect overcoming saints who will be raptured.

There are real problems with this view. First of all, the Scripture said, "She being with child cried, travailing in birth, and pained to be delivered." The church is to be the virgin bride of Christ. If she's pregnant, she's in trouble. Secondly, I reject the man Child as being an elite kind of saint, who only will be raptured. This teaching contradicts the Spirit of grace.

I believe that the identity of the woman as Israel is definite. There is a third view that the man Child is the 144,000 who, in the midst of the tribulation, will be caught up to their thrones and take their places in the heavenly scene. At that time Israel flees into the wilderness where God has prepared a place for her. He will feed her there for three and a half years, the last half of the great tribulation period.

When Jesus was talking to the Jews, the disciples said, "Lord, what will be the sign of Your coming, and of the end of the world?" One of the signs that Jesus gave them was: When you see the abomination of desolation, spoken of by Daniel the prophet, stand in the holy place, then flee into the wilderness. If you're on your housetop, don't even bother to stop for your goods, but get out as fast as you can (Matthew 24:3, 15–17).

This particular time of abomination when Israel flees was spoken of by Daniel the prophet (Daniel 9:27), and it is spoken of here in Revelation 12.

When the Antichrist comes on the scene, he'll have a false prophet who will lead the world to worship the Antichrist. Then an image of the Antichrist will be set up in the Holy of Holies of the rebuilt temple. This blasphemous image profanes again the temple of God as did Antiochus Epiphanes (c. 168 BC), who was a type of the Antichrist.

One thousand, two hundred and ninety days after Antichrist stops the oblations and brings this horrible blasphemy, Jesus is coming again with power and great glory and with His church to establish the kingdom of God upon the earth (Daniel 12:11).

REVELATION 12:7-17

At the time of this desecration of the rebuilt temple "there was war in heaven: Michael and his angels fought against the dragon; and the dragon fought and his angels" (Rev. 12:7). Those angels which kept not their first estate, which chose to rebel with Satan, are fighting on the side of Satan against Michael and the angels of God.

> And [Satan] prevailed not; neither was their place found any more in heaven. And the great dragon was cast out, that old serpent, called the Devil, and Satan, which deceived the whole world he was cast out into the earth, and his angels were cast out with him (Rev. 12:89).

It's interesting that God in His toleration has allowed Satan to be around for so long, but the day will come when God casts him out.

At that day, John said,

> I heard a loud voice saying in heaven, Now is come salvation, and strength, and the kingdom of our God, and the power of his Christ: for the accuser of our brethren is cast down, which accused them before our God day and night. And they overcame him by the blood of the Lamb, and by the word of their testimony; and they loved not their lives unto the death (Rev. 12:10–11).

The victory over Satan was through the blood of Jesus Christ. That is our victory over Satan today—the blood of Christ, the word of our testimony, and our total dedication by loving not our life unto death.

"Therefore rejoice, you heavens, and you that dwell in them" (Rev. 12:12). What a glorious time when Satan is finally booted out of heaven. Rejoice, he's gone! Rotten accuser! But, "Woe to the inhabiters of the earth and of the sea! for the devil is come down unto you, having great wrath, because he knows that he has but a short time" (Rev. 12:12).

He knows it's over. He's ready now to rip things up in this last three and a half year period.

> And when the dragon saw that he was cast unto the earth, he persecuted the woman [Israel] which brought forth the man Child. And to the woman were given two wings of a great eagle, that she might fly into the wilderness, into her place, where she is nourished for a time, and times, and half a time, from the face of the serpent (Rev. 12:13–14).

A "time" is a year. "Times" would be two years. "Half a time" would be half a year. So, the woman is protected for three and a half years "from the face of the serpent."

> And the serpent cast out of his mouth water as a flood after the woman ["flood" symbolizes an army], that he might cause her to be carried away by the flood. And the earth helped the woman, and the earth opened her mouth, and swallowed up the flood which the dragon cast out of his mouth. And the dragon was angry with the woman, and went to make war with the remnant of her seed, which keep the commandments of God, and have the testimony of Jesus Christ (Rev. 12:15–17).

This place in the wilderness is actually the ancient rock city of Petra where the Jews will flee during this last three and a half year period. Petra is an impregnable fortress that lies back in the Ha'arva valley in Jordan, south of the Dead Sea.

In Isaiah, God declares that Sela, which is Petra, will be the place of shelter for the Jews when they are cast out. God commands those of Jordan to open their doors and to receive His people and to give them shelter until the indignation be past (Isaiah 16:1–4).

CHAPTER 13
THE ANTICHRIST

E verybody today throughout the world longs for peace. We're tired of war. We know that war doesn't accomplish anything. It saps the country of its economy and strength. Even as a conqueror we feel guilty, because we realize that war is no way to settle differences.

People who are intelligent ought to be able to sit down and intelligently communicate with each other and solve their differences and problems. It doesn't seem reasonable for rational, sane men to create weapons of mass destruction to use on other human beings. It doesn't seem right to allocate billions of tax dollars to build and design mighty arsenals for the purpose of destroying people. Deep down in our hearts we want peace. All over the world people want peace. Then why do we fight? Why are there wars? You would think that we could finally achieve a standard of development where wars would be eliminated.

But, unfortunately, there are two more tremendous wars that the earth will experience before we can finally discover peace.

Plans are being drawn for the next-to-last battle. I expect it to take place at any time. The fuse is already lit. I don't know how much time there is before it blows up.

An alliance of nations from the north, including Turkey and Iran, are going to invade Israel according to Ezekiel 38 and 39. This will be prior to the last battle. When this alliance of nations begins to push Israel back and defeat her forces, God is going to step in and fight for Israel. He will destroy five-sixths of the army. This will allow a federation of ten nations to rise into power in Western Europe and to exercise immediate world influence and control.

At that time a man will come on the scene with some fantastic answers for peace. He'll be like a magician in his ability to get nations and people together. He'll sign a covenant with the nation Israel, and Israel will accept it. He'll build his own powerful economic bloc and monetary system. All the world will wonder after this man and follow him and his schemes and programs. This man is the Antichrist.

Those who refuse to follow him willingly will be subject to attack, and he will subdue them. Egypt will be one of the nations against which he'll move. While he's moving against Egypt, Red China and the nations of the East (Japan and India) will send their forces to invade the European continent by coming through the land of Israel. The River Euphrates will be dried up to prepare the way for the kings of the east (literally "the kings of the rising sun") (Rev. 16:12). Allied with the king of the north, Russia, they will marshal their millions of people and arm them to move against this confederation of European nations. This final war is the Battle of Armageddon.

REVELATION 13:1

The Beast—

And I stood upon the sand of the sea, and I saw a beast rise up out of the sea, having seven heads and ten horns, and upon his horns ten crowns, and upon his heads the name of blasphemy (Rev. 13:1).

This beast out of the sea is the Antichrist. He will rise out of the ten nations of the Common Market, the rejuvenated and renewed Roman Empire. This description of the beast takes us back to Nebuchadnezzar's dream of the great image with ten toes of iron and clay (Daniel 2).

Nebuchadnezzar, the King of Babylon, had a dream. In his dream he saw a great idol with a head of gold, breast and arms of silver, a stomach of brass, legs of iron, and feet of iron and clay. The feet had ten toes of iron and clay mixture. A rock not cut with hands came out of the mountain. It smote this great image in its feet, and the whole image fell. This rock began to grow until it filled the whole earth.

Nebuchadnezzar had two problems when he woke up. First, he couldn't remember his dream. Second, he knew that it terrified him because he didn't understand it. So, he called all his wise men and counselors and demanded that they tell him both what he dreamed and what it meant.

They kept stalling and said, "There's no way we can tell what your dream meant if we don't know what you dreamed! Tell us what you dreamed, then we'll tell you what it meant." He said, "I can't remember. But if you're really such wise men, tell me what I dreamed! If you don't, I'm going to have you all killed." Finally, they gave up trying to give him the answers, and so he gave the order for them to be killed.

When Daniel heard about the edict of King Nebuchadnezzar, he sent him a message. "Tell the king to settle down. I'll come and tell him what he dreamed and what it meant.

Meanwhile, Daniel told his friends, "We'd better pray. We're on the spot now!" While praying, God came to Daniel and revealed the dream and gave him the interpretation.

Daniel went to the king. "Nebuchadnezzar, you have seen in a dream the kingdoms of this world." Nebuchadnezzar had a dream which was a prophecy of what would happen to the kingdoms of the Gentile world. And Daniel described the dream as Nebuchadnezzar had seen it—this great image, made up of various metals, which was destroyed by a huge rock out of the mountain.

Then Daniel said, "This is what your dream meant. You, Nebuchadnezzar, are the head of gold. God has given you the kingdoms of the world. You're ruling over them, but your kingdom will be replaced by the Medo-Persian empire, the breast and arms of silver. But that kingdom will be replaced by the Grecian empire, the stomach of brass. And that empire will be replaced by the Roman empire, the legs of iron."

The *final* world-ruling kingdom is yet to arise. These are the ten toes of the iron and clay mixture. A federation of ten nations associated with the old Roman empire—or at least comprising many of the nations of the Roman empire because of the iron substance mixed within the image's feet—will arise as a world ruling empire.

I definitely believe that the European Community nations are a presage of this ten-nation federation. It's extremely interesting as we watch the events that God spoke of thousands of years ago take place in our daily newspapers.

Out of this ten-nation federation there shall arise a very powerful leader. He will be vested with all the powers of Satan and able to deceive the nations by his miracles in bringing peaceful solutions to the troubled world. This ten-nation federation will come to an end as this rock not cut with hands comes out of the mountain. It will smite the image in its feet and destroy it. The rock is Jesus Christ.

Nebuchadnezzar saw a vision of the second coming of Jesus Christ to establish His kingdom upon the earth. Daniel 2:44 declares, "And in the days of these ten kings shall the God of heaven set up a kingdom that shall never be destroyed." When Christ comes again, the Gentile rule will be over. Jesus will establish His kingdom which will fill the entire earth. It will be the most glorious age that man has ever known. We are coming to a golden age—the age when Jesus Christ rules and reigns. I'm waiting for the Age of Jesus!

REVELATION 13:2-4

> The beast which I saw was like a leopard, and his feet were as the feet of a bear, and his mouth as the mouth of a lion: and the dragon gave him his power, and his throne, and great authority (Rev. 13:2).

Satan promised to give Jesus the kingdoms of this earth if only He would bow down and worship him. Satan said, "All these things will I give You, if You will fall down and worship me" (Matthew 4:9).

Now, Satan turns the kingdoms of the world over to the Antichrist, which indicates that Satan is still in control of the world. He is still the prince of this world and the god of this age. He has the world under his control. So, don't blame God for the calamities in the world around you. It is Satan's world. He has the authority now. He's the one who is ruling—and with man's consent in many cases.

And I saw one of his heads as it were wounded to death: and his deadly wound was healed: and all the world wondered after the beast. And they worshiped the dragon which gave power unto the beast: and they worshiped the beast, saying, Who is like unto the beast? Who is able to make war with him? (Rev. 13:3–4).

The Antichrist will be the victim of an assassination attempt in which, it seems, his right eye will be put out and his arm paralyzed (Zechariah 11:17). Yet, though he appears to be dead, he will be revived. All the world will wonder after him when it sees his power. People will ask, "Who is able to make war with this fellow?" He'll become a superman in the eyes of the world.

And then the Bible says that they will worship the dragon—Satan worship. That's unthinkable, isn't it? Yet, it's amazing how many people are now consciously worshiping Satan today. Even here in the United States, satanic cults are widespread. The Antichrist, of course, will be an instrument through which they will worship him.

REVELATION 13:5-15

And there was given unto him a mouth speaking great things and blasphemies; and power was given unto him to continue forty and two months. And he opened his mouth in blasphemy against God, to blaspheme his name, and his tabernacle, and them that dwell in heaven. And it was given to him to make war with the saints [Israel], and to overcome them: and power was given to him over all the kindreds, and tongues, and nations (Rev. 13:5–7).

Those who use this Scripture in an attempt to prove that the church will be on earth during the great tribulation period fail to note that the Antichrist overcomes the saints, which is contrary to the concept of the "super saint" usually accompanying this heresy. It is also contrary to the statement of Jesus in Matthew 16:18, concerning His church, that the gates of hell would not prevail against it.

All that dwell upon the earth shall worship him, whose names are not written in the book of life of the Lamb slain from the foundation of the world. If any man has an ear, let him hear. He that leads into captivity shall go into captivity: he that kills with the sword must be killed with the sword. Here is the patience and the faith of the saints. And I beheld another beast [the false prophet who leads the world to worship the Antichrist] coming up out of the earth; and he had two horns like a lamb [he looked like a lamb but]...he spoke as a dragon (Rev.13:8–11).

And he exercised all the power of the first beast before him, and caused the earth and them which dwell therein to worship the first beast, whose deadly wound was healed. And he does great wonders, so that he makes fire come down from heaven on the earth in the sight of men [mimicking the work of the two witnesses], and deceived them that dwell on the earth by the means of those miracles which he had power to do in the sight of the beast; saying to them that dwell on the earth, that they should make an image to the beast, which had the wound by a sword, and did live (Rev. 13:12–14).

The false prophet promotes the idea of making an image of the beast that the world might worship.

And he had power to give life unto the image of the beast, that the image of the beast should both speak, and cause that as many as would not worship the image of the beast should be killed (Rev. 13:15).

This power to give life sounds like a computer which is fed information and has the capacity of speaking and declaring certain things. We're arriving to that point in our modern computerized society.

REVELATION 13:16-18

"666"—

And he caused all, both small and great, rich and poor, free and bond, to receive a mark in their right hand, or in their foreheads: and that no man might [be able to] buy or sell, except he that had the mark, or the name of the beast, or the number of his name. Here is wisdom. Let him who has understanding count the number of the beast: for it is the number of a man; and his number is Six hundred and sixty six [666] (Rev.13:16–18).

I've started a collection of items branded 666. I have a little tag from a shirt made in Japan with a 666 trademark. I have a large bag of fertilizer made in West Germany with 666 in big numbers on it. Why would people choose that number to brand things?

But even more interesting is the concept of buying and selling with numbers and setting up the whole monetary system on a mark and number basis rather than on the cash and check basis such as we are using today. No one will be able to buy or sell without a number.

Bankers are already planning to get rid of money and implementing a totally computerized monetary system. There are banks that offer this service even at the present time in California. An advertisement several years ago in the *Los Angeles Times* said, "In the beginning there was money, and it was good. But now a better system." The ad told how to have your checks credited to your account in the bank and have your bills sent there. The bank takes care of all your bills. You don't have to use your money anymore. You can use your charge card for everything you buy or sell. You'll never see your checkbook and never have to bother with money again. We're coming closer to it.

There's only one problem with this system—stolen credit cards. So, they'll have to figure out a solution, but there's an easy solution to that. All you have to do is implant a microchip with a number under the skin on the person's hand or forehead. You can easily make purchases with the microchip. No one's going to cut off your hand or your head to steal your number. It'll be a very easy way of identification. No one will be able to buy or sell without it, just as the Scripture said. We can see the whole thing shaping up.

CHAPTER 14

FINAL WARNING

REVELATION 14:1-5

I n Revelation 14 we see the 144,000 again. Now they're on Mount Zion with Christ. "I looked, and, lo, a Lamb stood on the mount Zion, and with him an hundred and forty four thousand, having his Father's name written in their foreheads. And I heard a voice from heaven, as the voice of many waters, and as the voice of a great thunder: and I heard the voice of harpers harping with their harps: and they sung as it were a new song before the throne, and before the four living creatures, and the elders: and no man could learn that song but the hundred and forty four thousand, which were redeemed from the earth.

These are they which were not defiled with women; for they are virgins. These are they which follow the Lamb wherever he goes. These were redeemed from among men, being the firstfruits unto God and to the Lamb (Rev. 14:1–4).

These, I believe, are Orthodox Jews who, sometime after the rapture of the church, come to the realization that Jesus Christ was indeed the Messiah. When the rest of their nation is deceived by the Antichrist, these people will start crying out against the alliance Israel makes with him. Of course, Elijah and the second prophet (perhaps Moses, Enoch, or Zerubbabel) will have returned as the two witnesses and will be bearing witness of Jesus Christ.

In the fifth trumpet judgment as the fifth angel sounded, John saw a star (Satan) falling from heaven unto the earth with the key to the *abyss*, the bottomless pit (Rev. 9). Satan opened the *abyss* and all these hellish creatures came out upon the earth. These creatures looked like locusts but had stingers like scorpions. They were commanded not to hurt the grass nor any green thing nor the trees but only those men which had not the seal of God in their foreheads. The 144,000 are marked and sealed by God so that they are not hurt by these remaining judgments coming upon the earth.

The 144,000 are found in typology in the Old Testament. At the time of Noah, God saw the earth and it was exceedingly wicked. He decided to destroy it. He saw only one man who was righteous, Noah, and commanded him to build an ark.

So, Noah built the ark and entered it with the animals. God shut the door and judgment came. Noah was spared because he was sealed by God in the ark (Genesis 6 & 7). Noah passed through the tribulation or judgment without being touched. He is a type of the 144,000.

Noah's great-grandfather, Enoch, walked with God; and he was not, for God took him (Genesis 5:24). Enoch is a type of the church walking with God who is raptured or taken out before the judgment ever comes.

There are many groups, as we mentioned before, seeking to identify themselves as the 144,000. Revelation 7 shows very plainly that these are actually Israelites—twelve thousand from each of the twelve tribes. The Jehovah's Witnesses jump on the verse "having their Father's name written in their foreheads." They say, "What is the Father's name? It's Jehovah." Thus, they are "Jehovah's" witnesses, which is their claim as the 144,000. But the name Jehovah, actually, is not a true name. Look it up in the dictionary. It's a mistake that has crept in. The name is actually YHWH.

The 144,000 are singing a song which is exclusively theirs. They are virgins. They do **follow** the Lamb wherever He goes. The church is the bride of Christ and she is **with** the Lamb and shall ever be with the Lamb. The 144,000 don't have as great a place in heaven as the body of Christ. So, I have no desire to be one of them. God has chosen a better place for me as a part of the Bride of Christ.

"And in their mouth was found no guile: for they are without fault before the throne of God" (Rev. 14:5).

That's exactly how I'm going to be before the throne of God. Jude said, "Now unto him who is able to keep you from falling, and to present you faultless before the presence of his glory with exceeding joy" (Jude 24).

When Jesus Christ presents me to the Father, I'll be without fault. Why? Because He has washed away all my sin and guilt. Not that I'm faultless—far from it! But that's the way Jesus is presenting me because of His work of grace within my life.

It's a tragedy that people clamor to be identified as the 144,000. They must have a persecution complex or a masochistic desire to be on the earth when the judgment of God comes. Even if I were to be spared the tribulation, just to see it around me would be horrible.

Rescued—There's an easy way to go and there's a tough way to go. If you want to play it tough, God will play it tough with you. God can get just as rough as you want. But know this—He's going to get you! Enough prayers have gone up for you. God isn't going to let you go. He'll get you sooner or later. Much better sooner than later.

That's what the Gospel is all about. That's why Jesus Christ suffered and died. Because God isn't willing that any should perish but that all should come to repentance (2 Peter 3:9).

For the joy of being able to forgive, the joy of being able to make you a totally new person, the kind of person God wants you to be, and the joy of being able to wash you from all your sins and all your past and all the guilt, He endured the cross, despising the shame (Hebrews 12:2).

God has done all these things to save you. If you're not saved, it isn't God's fault. There's no one to blame but yourself. Many of you like to blame other people. You say, "There are so many hypocrites in church!" It's true that there are hypocrites in church. Let me tell you something: there aren't any hypocrites in heaven. If you hate hypocrites so much, then you better change your ways or you'll be surrounded by them.

You don't have anyone to blame but yourself. God loves you and wants to show you that love. God wants to wash away your sins, and He's ready to do it.

God is ready now to put His mark on you. The 144,000 will be given the seal of God on their foreheads. But God wants to seal you today. He wants to put His mark of ownership on you today. The seal He wants to put on you is His Holy Spirit. The church is sealed with the Holy Spirit, the down payment until the redemption of the purchased possession (Ephesians 1:13–14).

You see, God bought me. Jesus Christ purchased me. I belong to Him. How do I know He'll carry out the deal? Because He's already made a down payment. He put His mark of ownership on me by giving me the gift of His Holy Spirit. God claims me as His. He has stamped me.

Knowing that I belong to God is so beautiful! Even though I may mess up at times, even though I may fail God at times, even though I don't live a perfect life all day long every day, still that seal is on me. I'm His property. I may stumble, fall, and get dirty, but He brings me in, cleans me up, and sets me on my feet again. It's so great to be God's child!

God wants to make you His child today. He wants to seal you. That's what the Gospel is all about. God can change your life. God will change your life if you'll just give Him the chance. God can make everything new. God can take away those old habits and those weaknesses. God can take away that sin from your life. God can change your very nature, your attitude, your heart. And He wants to.

REVELATION 14:6-13

The Angels' Messages—

And I saw another angel fly in the midst of heaven, having the everlasting Gospel to preach unto them that dwell on the earth, and to every nation, and kindred, and tongue, and people (Rev. 14:6).

Jesus said that the Gospel shall be preached for a witness to all nations, "and then shall the end come" (Matthew 24:14). For a long time many people have been saying, "The Lord can't come yet, because the Gospel hasn't been preached as a witness to all nations."

There were great missionary drives whose theme was "Bring Back the King." In other words, get the Gospel out into all the world to hasten the day and bring back the King, Jesus Christ. "He can't come as long as you're sitting back and not supporting missionary work!" I am all for missionary work and supporting missions, it is a part of the great commission of Jesus to the church to go into all the world and preach the Gospel to every creature. I do not believe the motive for missions is to make it possible for Jesus to return for His church. This has been used as a great challenge and motivation for missions. However, here we are told that God will use supernatural beings to proclaim the Gospel.

These supernatural messengers proclaim God's Gospel "with a loud voice, [saying,] Fear God, and give glory to him; for the hour of his judgment is come: and worship him that made heaven, and earth, and the sea, and the fountains of waters" (Rev. 14:7).

They are calling upon people to worship God, to reverence God, to give glory to Him for the hour of His judgment has come.

And there followed another angel, saying, Babylon is fallen, is fallen, that great city, because she made all the nations drink of the wine of the wrath of her fornication (Rev. 14:8).

This will be further explained in Revelation 17.

The third angel followed them, saying with a loud voice, If any man worship the beast and his image, and receive his mark in his forehead, or in his hand, the same shall drink of the wine of the wrath of God, which is poured out without mixture into the cup of his indignation; and he shall be tormented with fire and brimstone in the presence of the holy angels, and in the presence of the Lamb: and the smoke of their torment ascends up for ever and ever: and they have no rest day nor night, who worship the beast and his image, and whosoever receives the mark of his name (Rev. 14:9–11)

Every person will be warned. If a person worships the Antichrist or worships his image or takes his mark, he will be in deliberate rebellion against God, even as man is in deliberate rebellion against God today. Here, God will be supernaturally warning men not to bow to the Antichrist. Yet, they will ignore God's warning and act in open defiance and rebellion against God. The Antichrist will be a man of blasphemy and make fun of all the declarations of these divine beings—even though they are declaring the punishment of God.

Many people would have me modify the punishment declared against the wicked. I can't. God has called me to declare His Word, not my opinion. The end of Revelation says,

> If any man shall add unto these things [the words of this book], God shall add unto him the plagues that are written in this book: and if any man shall take away from the words of the book of this prophecy, God shall take away his part out of the book of life (Rev. 22:18–19).

Please don't ask me to take away from or add to the Revelation, because I have no intention of doing it. The plight of the ungodly, those who worship the Antichrist, is a horrible thing to contemplate. Yet, God has said it and I cannot modify it.

> Here is the patience of the saints: here are they that keep the commandments of God, and the faith of Jesus. And I heard a voice from heaven saying unto me, Write, Blessed are the dead which die in the Lord from henceforth: Yea, says the Spirit, that they may rest from their labors; and their works do follow them (Rev. 14:12–13).

At this time, death will be preferable to life. Those put to death by the Antichrist for not worshiping him or taking his mark will actually have a better place than those who live. Happy are the dead who die in the Lord, because they've ceased from this horrible tribulation, and their works do follow them.

REVELATION 14:14-20

A Vision of Armageddon—Prior to the return of Jesus Christ and the establishment of the kingdom of God upon the earth, the world is going to experience a blood bath. God will unleash fully and completely these powers of darkness and the forces of Satan that will wreak havoc throughout the earth.

John received a vision of this terrible Battle of Armageddon about which we have heard so much. The valley of Megiddo is where this great battle will be fought.

> I looked, and behold a white cloud, and upon the cloud One sat like unto the Son of man, having on His head a golden crown, and in His hand a sharp sickle. And another angel came out of the temple, crying with a loud voice to Him that sat on the cloud, Thrust in Your sickle, and reap: for the time is come for You to reap; for the harvest of the earth is ripe. And He that sat on the cloud thrust in his sickle on the earth; and the earth was reaped.

> And another angel came out of the temple which is in heaven, he also having a sharp sickle. And another angel came out from the altar, which had power over fire; and cried with a loud cry to him that had the sharp sickle, saying, Thrust in your sharp sickle, and gather the clusters of the vine of the earth; for her grapes are fully ripe. And the angel thrust in his sickle into the earth and gathered the vine of the earth, and cast it into the great winepress of the wrath of God. And the winepress was trodden without the city, and blood came out of the winepress, even unto the horse bridles, by the space of a thousand and six hundred furlongs (Rev. 14:14–20).

This describes the valley of Megiddo as filled with blood from the great Battle of Armageddon.

In Revelation 16 we will see three unclean spirits who gather together the kings of the earth (v. 13–14). The Antichrist will establish his power and his authority through a united European national front and will develop tremendous military power. The people of the world will be saying, "Who is able to make war with the 'beast'?"

The nations of the East, probably a combination of Japan, China, and India, will launch an attack on the Antichrist by coming down across from the east through the dried-up River Euphrates. They will meet the forces of Europe, with which the United States will probably be allied, in that great battle in the valley of Megiddo. God's wrath and indignation, the day of His vengeance, shall come.

The world has one great war yet to endure—the war to end all wars. The rebellious nations of man will be as ripe grapes trodden and bursting. The slaughter that will take place is too frightening to imagine. Just be thankful that you're not going to be around!

CHAPTER 15

THE PLAGUES
ARE COMING!

The fifteenth chapter of Revelation is, as it were, an introduction to Revelation 16. It sets the background scene from which the judgments in Revelation 16 will emerge, and brings us to the final judgment of God upon the earth prior to the return of Jesus Christ.

There is one aspect of the book of Revelation that sometimes makes it difficult to understand or follow—the related events do not always follow a chronological order. Many times John will describe the overall scene and then return to fill in the details and amplify some of the earlier descriptions. Such is the case with Revelation 15 and 16. These are fill-in chapters which add further details to events already described.

In Revelation 10 we came to the second coming of Jesus Christ. We also read of it in Revelation 14. However, the events in Revelation 15 and 16 will be taking place before the Lord's second coming. These are the details of God's judgments to be poured upon this earth very soon because of the rejection of His love and grace. God is going to purge the world before Jesus comes to reign again.

Chapter 15 shows us what is happening in heaven while Revelation 16 describes the corresponding events taking place upon the earth during the great tribulation period. The church shall be in heaven with Christ at this time.

REVELATION 15:1-3

John said, "I saw another sign in heaven" (Rev. 15:1). The word *sign* means "wonder" or "miracle." The Bible speaks of the

Lord working signs and wonders (Acts 2:19, et al). Now there is another miracle in heaven... "great and marvelous, seven angels having the seven last plagues; for in them is filled up the wrath of God" (Rev. 15:1).

The seven last plagues will complete the judgment of God against this Christ-rejecting world. It will also complete God's purging process. Once this is over, Christ will come back with His church to set up His kingdom, and the righteous government of God over the earth will begin.

"I saw as it were a sea of glass mingled with fire" (Rev. 15:2). Before the throne of God in heaven there appears a "sea of glass." In Revelation 4 John said the sea of glass was clear "like unto crystal" (Rev. 4:6). But here John sees it as "mingled with fire." This could be a foreboding of the impending fiery judgment when the seven vials are poured upon the earth.

John saw those "that had gotten the victory over the beast [Antichrist], and over his image, and over his mark, and over the number of his name, stand on the sea of glass, having the harps of God" (Rev. 15:2).

This is not the church standing in heaven on this sea of glass. It is probably the 144,000 who were sealed in Revelation 7. These have the victory over the Antichrist and over his image. The church will never see the Antichrist. As a matter of fact, he can't be revealed until the church is taken out of the way, until that which hinders is removed (2 Thessalonians 2:3–8). Then the Antichrist shall come forth with all his lying wonders and deceit, deceiving if possible even the very "elect." Many Jews will be drawn into a pact with him.

John sees the group standing with the harps of God. "And they sing the song of Moses" (Rev. 15:3). This causes me to believe that they are the 144,000 of Israel. The song of Moses is the song of Israel's deliverance out of Egypt. The Jews escaped from their enemy when they reached the other side of the Red Sea and the waters closed on the Egyptian army. The Jews sang the song of Moses, the song of victory and deliverance (Exodus 15:1–21).

Here, they have also been delivered from the hand of their enemy, the Antichrist. So, they sing "the song of Moses the servant of God, and the song of the Lamb [the victory through Jesus Christ], saying, Great and marvelous are Your works, Lord God Almighty; just and true are Your ways, O King of saints" (Rev. 15:3). This song of praise unto God tells of the great and marvelous works of God.

Notice the proclamation that the works of God are just and true. God is absolutely just, far more than we could ever be. It's stupid for us to challenge the justice of God. "I don't see how God can..." We act as if we're purer or more just than God. That's ridiculous. Yet, we often hear people challenging His justice.

Satan is constantly challenging the justice of God. But God is and will always be absolutely fair. The 144,000, witnessing part of God's judgment, are proclaiming in song, "Just and true is the King of saints."

REVELATION 15:4-8

Who shall not fear You, O Lord, and glorify Your name? for You only are holy: for all nations shall come and worship before You; for You judgments are made manifest (Rev. 15:4).

Who shall not come and worship? All the nations will come and worship before Christ when He returns again. He'll rule over all the nations and "every knee shall bow... every tongue shall confess that Jesus Christ is Lord, to the glory of God the Father" (Philippians 2:10–11).

And after that I looked, and, behold, the temple of the tabernacle of the testimony in heaven was opened: And the seven angels came out of the temple, having the seven plagues, clothed in pure and white linen, and having their breasts girded with golden girdles. And one of the four living creatures [the cherubim] gave unto the seven angels seven golden vials full of the wrath of God, who lives for ever and ever. And the temple was filled with smoke from the glory of God, and from his power; and no man was able to enter into the temple, till the seven plagues of the seven angels were fulfilled (Rev. 15:5–8).

Interestingly enough, there is a temple in heaven. The earthly tabernacle that God commanded Moses to build was patterned after the heavenly temple and included the various courts, the holy place, the Holy of Holies in the center of the temple where God dwelled, and the mercy seat (Hebrews 8:5). Jesus, as our High Priest, did not enter into the earthly tabernacle built by hands but entered into that heavenly place to offer His blood as an atoning sacrifice for our sin (Hebrews 9:24).

John now watches as the seven angels come forth and the cherubim give them the seven golden vials full of the wrath of God. In Revelation 16 these seven angels pour out the vials of God's wrath upon the earth—the plagues which are the final judgment before the return of Jesus Christ in glory.

CHAPTER 16

A WORLD OF DESPAIR

I find it difficult to discuss the judgment of God because it isn't a very savory subject, nor is it an idealistic theme I can really get into. I would much rather present one hundred messages on the love of God than one on the wrath of God, for God is love (1 John 4:8). How thankful I am that I've experienced the love of God and that God's love is being extended to every one of you.

But, it is also true that if you rebel against God and want nothing to do with Him, then you will experience that other side of God's nature—His judgment.

The Bible declares,

For we know Him who has said, Vengeance belongs unto Me, I will recompense, says the Lord... It is a fearful thing to fall into the hands of the living God (Hebrews 10:30–31).

In Revelation 16 we read of some of these "fearful" things. I'd like to skip over them if I could, because it's a tough scene that's coming. Thank God I don't have to be around to see it. I would hope to God that no one was around. I would hope to God that the whole world accepted Christ and the whole tribulation was unnecessary. That would be so great!

"O God, we've been such fools! We've messed things up so bad, Lord! We give up! It's a mess! Take it, Lord!" If man would realize how foolish and stupid he's been, and how he's allowed greed to destroy him, and would just turn it all over to the Lord—then we would not have to experience Revelation 16.

You don't have to experience Revelation 16. Don't build a case against God because He tells you that He'll do these things. You don't have to be around when He does them. Many people fault God because of what He said He would do to the sinner. Well, you don't have to be a sinner.

You don't have to experience God's judgment. God doesn't want you to. In fact, He so loved you that He made arrangements for you to miss all these things. In order that He might have many sons, you and me included, He gave His only begotten Son that, if we believe, we wouldn't perish but have everlasting life (John 3:16). It cost Him an awful lot to spare you. It cost Him His only Son.

God didn't send His Son into the world to condemn the world "but that the world through him might be saved. He that believes on Him is not condemned: but he that believes not is condemned already, because he has not believed in the name of the only begotten Son of God. And this is the condemnation, that light is come into the world," but you rejected the light (John 3:17–19).

You may have all kinds of arguments for being the way you are. "I didn't have a chance! My father beat me when I was a child." You may have all kinds of phony excuses to offer God for the things that you've done, but you have no excuse for rejecting God's light in Jesus Christ. God has declared that the reason you will not come to the light is that you love darkness rather than light, because your deeds are evil. You may offer many excuses, but God knows the real reason.

You say, "There are so many churches! I don't know what church to believe." God didn't tell you to believe in any church. God said to believe in His Son.

"There are so many hypocrites!" God didn't tell you to believe in the hypocrites. He told you to believe in His Son.

For those of you who love the darkness, who rebel against God, who just close the door to God's love, and want nothing to do with God—unfortunately, God will honor your request. He'll withdraw Himself completely from you.

The absence of God's love is hell. If God would ever withdraw His love completely from this earth, it would be hell on earth. And that's exactly what it's going to be! That's what we read about in Revelation. With God's love having been withdrawn, the forces of hell—these diabolic forces that are now restrained because of the power of the Spirit of God working in the church—will be unleashed.

Revelation 16 depicts a world without God, a world without hope, a world of despair.

REVELATION 16:1-4

In Revelation 15 the temple of God in heaven was filled with smoke. No one was allowed to enter in until the seven vials were completely poured out upon the earth.

In Revelation 16 John said,

I heard a great voice out of the temple saying to the seven angels, Go your ways, and pour out the vials of the wrath of God upon the earth (Rev. 16:1).

The voice out of the temple is perhaps even the voice of God commanding the seven angels to go their way and pour out these vials of wrath upon the earth.

The first went, and poured out his vial upon the earth; and there fell a noisome and grievous sore upon the men which had the mark of the beast, and upon them which worshiped his image (Rev. 16:2).

This takes us back to the Antichrist. He is the man of sin who will soon be coming on the world scene bringing tremendous solutions for the world problems, bringing nations together in peaceful co-existence, establishing a new monetary system, and creating signs and wonders. All the world will wonder after this man and say, "There's no one like him. He's really sharp. He's really got the answers!" He will create this new monetary system. No one will be able to buy or sell except he has the mark and the number of this man either on his wrist or on his forehead (Rev. 13:17).

Already we're conditioned to buy with numbers. Credit cards and debit cards are getting more and more popular every day. Money is almost becoming a thing of the past.

Upon those who took his mark and worshiped the image in the temple there will come a noisome and grievous sore (literally, a running sore like a boil or an open ulcer). It's interesting that some of the side effects from the nuclear blast on Hiroshima were radiation burns like running ulcers which could not heal. More people died as the result of the radiation after effects than by the initial nuclear blast. Whether or not radioactivity will cause the sores I don't know.

> The second angel poured out his vial upon the sea [probably the Mediterranean Sea]; and it became as the blood of a dead man: and every living thing died in the sea (Rev. 16:3).

The sea becomes polluted by some method. It becomes like the blood of a dead man and destroys all life within it.

> The third angel poured out his vial upon the rivers and fountains of waters; and they became blood (Rev. 16:4).

REVELATION 16:5-7

> And I heard the angel of the waters say, You are righteous, O Lord, who is, and was, and shall be, because You have judged thus. For they have shed the blood of saints and prophets, and You have given them blood to drink; for they are worthy. And I heard another out of the altar say, Even so, Lord God Almighty, true and righteous are Your judgments (Rev. 16:5–7).

"But Why Does God?"—When God begins to judge, every transgression and disobedience will receive a just recompense of reward. The Antichrist and his followers have killed the saints and blasphemed God. They beheaded everyone who refused to take the mark of the beast. They destroyed and killed the two prophets that

God sent. They shed so much innocent blood that now the Lord gives them blood to drink. He changes the fresh water supplies into blood. Men turn on a spigot in their houses to get a drink and bloody water pours out.

The angels said, "That serves them right. They've shed the blood of the innocent and You've given them blood to drink. That's very fitting to their crimes." Even the voice from out of the altar in heaven says, "True and righteous are Your judgments, O God." God will not judge any man unfairly. No man will be able to point a finger at God and say, "You weren't fair."

You don't have to stand before the judgment seat of God if Jesus is your Savior. If He's not, you won't have a chance. You may con a lot of people, you may live by your wits, and you may be able to talk yourself out of just about any situation, but you'll not be able to talk your way out of this. You may plead, "I didn't have a chance! Here's what really happened." You may go on with a long spiel, but God knows your heart. He knows your very motive. He could play back the whole scene on a screen and show you your motivations. The Bible says that everything is open and revealed before Him with whom we have to deal (Luke 12:2). There'll be no conning God. Holy and righteous are His judgments.

What about that man who has never heard about Jesus Christ? When we see God's disposition in these cases, we'll say, "Right on! True and righteous, Lord, are Your judgments." Never fear—God will be righteous and fair when He judges.

Satan is constantly challenging the justice of God. He would have you believe that God isn't fair. This was his accusation of God to Adam and Eve in the Garden. "God doesn't want you to eat of that tree. He knows that if you eat of it you'll be as wise as He is. He's just trying to protect Himself. He's really not fair" (Genesis 3:4–5).

Constantly, we hear people challenging the fairness or the justice of God. "How can a loving God…?" "Why would a God of love…?"

God is absolutely just. Even when these judgments are being poured out there will be the confirmation of the righteousness of God's judgment. And what God does will be absolutely fair. Remember that.

REVELATION 16:8-11

The fourth angel poured out his vial upon the sun; and power was given unto him to scorch men with fire. And men were scorched with great heat, and blasphemed the name of God, who has power over these plagues: and they repented not to give Him glory (Rev. 16:8–9).

Turning on the Heat—Actually, it's extremely interesting that scientists are now crying grave warnings concerning the ozone blanket around the earth. Ozone is a very unstable gas, and the chlorofluorocarbons in aerosol cans rise into the atmosphere and upset this ozone blanket. The supersonic transport planes can also destroy the ozone layer above the earth.

This layer of ozone gas around the earth protects us from harmful rays. Without the ozone protection the ultraviolet rays of the sun would not be filtered out. Some scientists suggest that in the future this ozone blanket will be depleted to the extent that stepping outdoors will be dangerous. Any exposure to the sun would cause extreme burns and "scorch men."

A nuclear warhead exploded in the atmosphere does more damage to the ozone gas than everything else combined. If nuclear weapons are used during the great tribulation, they'll have their own detrimental effect on this ozone layer. This plague could also be caused by a nova or supernova condition. This is a stellar phenomenon in which a star suddenly seems to explode; e.g., a star may increase from fifteenth magnitude to negative three magnitude in two or three nights. It expands and grows brighter, and then dims out. In fact, some stars actually disappear.

It is very possible that our own star, the sun, will go into a nova or supernova condition when the fourth angel pours out his vial. I've been in the desert when it was 125 degrees, and that was hot. If our sun suddenly increased in intensity, it would get much hotter than that. The devastating heat would scorch men and parch the earth.

> The fifth angel poured out his vial upon the throne of the beast; and his kingdom was full of darkness [as though the sun did have a nova condition and darkness followed this brilliant display]; and they gnawed their tongues for pain (Rev. 16:10).

Their pain could be from the first vial with the boils that break out all over men or due to the tremendous sunburn blisters all over their bodies. But, as the result of these things, the people's hearts are hardened and, instead of repenting, they "blasphemed the God of heaven because of their pains and their sores, and repented not of their deeds" (Rev. 16:11).

The strange stupidity of man! When the judgments begin to come, rather than repenting, men are blaspheming God and blaming Him for their calamities.

Why is it that man always wants to blame God for his calamities? We do the most stupid things. We defy the rules and the laws of God. Then we want to blame God for the suffering that our actions entail. Here, men curse God because of their pains and sores.

REVELATION 16:12

> The sixth angel poured out his vial upon the great river Euphrates; and the water thereof was dried up, that the way of the kings of the east might be prepared (Rev. 16:12).

The great River Euphrates runs about eighteen hundred miles long. It is three to twelve miles wide with an average depth of thirty feet. The Euphrates is a natural barrier between the Eastern and the Western empires. The same Russian engineers who worked on the Aswan Dam in Egypt have built a great dam in Syria across the river Euphrates. The nations down-river on the Euphrates are quite upset that the river can be dammed up. It is extremely interesting

that Revelation talks about the River Euphrates being stopped up
to prepare the way for the kings of the east. We see how this could
become a reality today.

The Aswan Dam is also described in Scripture. Isaiah said that
they shall dam up the great river in Egypt. Then he describes all the
ecological catastrophes that would result as the Nile River is
dammed up (Isaiah 19:5–10).

Just as Isaiah predicted, it has happened. The fishing industry
along the coast has been wiped out. The saltwater intrusion has
destroyed more farmland than was gained by this Aswan project.
Vast, unexpected ecological problems have been created. These are
all described in Isaiah. If the Egyptians had only read Isaiah they
never would have built the dam. It's interesting how far the
prophecies of God are actually ahead of these modern
developments.

REVELATION 16:13-17

> I saw three unclean spirits like frogs come out of the
> mouth of the dragon [Satan], and out of the mouth of the
> beast [Antichrist], and out of the mouth of the false
> prophet [the one leading the world to worship the
> Antichrist] (Rev. 16:13).

I don't know why, but it seems that a person's spirit leaves his
body through the mouth. The Hebrew word for *spirit* is "ruach,"
which also means "breath." God breathed into Adam and he
became a living soul. Many who have had experiences of dying and
being brought back to life remember in their death a consciousness
of the spirit leaving through the mouth. When Jesus cast out
demons, many times great cries were let out.

The unclean spirits look like frogs and come forth out of the
mouth of Satan, the mouth of the Antichrist, and the mouth of the
false prophet.

> For they are the spirits of devils, working miracles, which
> go forth unto the kings of the earth and of the whole

world, to gather them to the battle of that great day of God Almighty (Rev. 16:14).

The kings of the earth will be driven by demon powers into this great Battle of Armageddon.

Hitler came very close to conquering the world. Only a few quirks kept him from completing his conquest, for the Nazis were very close to possessing the nuclear bomb. Had Hitler been able to develop a nuclear weapon before we did, the whole situation would have been different. You'd be living under the control of a madman.

Hitler was guided by men who were masters in the occult. These masters who controlled Hitler moved to South America after the fall of the Third Reich. These men, the masterminds behind the Third Reich, were themselves controlled by Satan.

This helps us to understand the Bible reference to these three unclean spirits who go forth and enter into the kings to draw them into battle. Men will be controlled by evil spirits even as Hitler was controlled by evil spirits. We see the result of one powerful man being under their control. We can only wonder what it will be like when three kings of the earth are demon-possessed and gather their armies together into this final conflict of Armageddon.

A Warning—At this point Jesus gives a warning. "Behold, I come as a thief. Blessed is he that watches, and keeps his garments, lest he walk naked, and they see his shame" (Rev. 16:15).

Jesus gives the warning in the midst of this great scene that He is coming again. He warns that He's coming quickly and as a thief. Those who are watching and those who are keeping their garments, so to speak, will not have to be here on the earth when this tribulation is taking place.

Jesus told the church, "Watch therefore, for you know neither the day nor the hour wherein the Son of man comes" (Matthew 25:13). Jesus said, "Pray always, that you may be accounted worthy to escape all these things that shall come to pass, and to stand before the Son of man" (Luke 21:36).

As Jesus is telling you these things that will be happening, again He warns you. "Watch and be ready for I'm coming as a thief." He said, "If the master of the house had known in what watch [hour] the thief would come, he would have watched" (Matthew 24:43). What I say unto one I say unto all. Watch!

"And he gathered them together into a place called in the Hebrew tongue Armageddon" (Rev. 16:16). This is in the Plain of Esdraelon and the Valley of Jezreel, the valley just below the ancient city of Megiddo.

> The seventh angel poured out his vial into the air; and there came a great voice out of the temple of heaven, from the throne, saying, It is finished (Rev. 16:17).

This same phrase was cried once before. When Jesus was hanging on the cross He cried with a loud voice, "It is finished" and then He died (John 19:30).

Jesus was talking about your salvation. It is a finished work. It was accomplished through His death upon the cross. The cry of Christ—"It is finished"—was a triumphant cry, not a cry of defeat. Jesus said, "No man takes my life from Me. I give My life" (John 10:18). He gave His life as a ransom for your sins. He has finished the work of redemption.

We find God crying the same phrase from the throne in heaven when the seventh vial is poured out. "It is finished." This is the final vial, the final outpouring of God's wrath upon the Christ rejecting world. "It is finished," the cry of Christ from the cross, brings victory and joy and salvation to our lives; and the second "It is finished" will proclaim the end of the wrath and judgment of God upon the earth.

REVELATION 16:18-21

> There were voices, and thunders, and lightnings; and there was a great earthquake, such as was not since men were upon the earth, so mighty an earthquake, and so great (Rev. 16:18).

God said, "Once again I'm going to shake the earth until everything that can be shaken shall be shaken, until only that which cannot be shaken shall be left" (Hebrews 12:26–27). One more tremendous earthquake.

However, this earthquake shall shake the entire world—an earthquake of greater intensity than man has ever experienced upon the earth.

This great earthquake interests me because many earthquakes are localized. In California we're very familiar with earthquakes, and we're familiar with each of the local faults. But here's an earthquake that is going to hit the entire earth. It will shake the mountains and the islands, and there will be no place of safety or refuge at this time.

> And the great city was divided into three parts, and the cities of the nations fell: and great Babylon came in remembrance before God, to give unto her the cup of the wine of the fierceness of His wrath. And every island fled away, and the mountains were not found. And there fell upon men a great hail out of heaven, every stone about the weight of a talent [about one hundred pounds]: and men blasphemed God because of the plague of the hail; for the plague thereof was exceeding great (Rev. 16:19–21).

When I was a child, the iceman used to sell blocks of ice for home iceboxes. The ice came in fifty and one hundred pound blocks. Can you imagine hailstones that huge falling?

We have had severe storms in Arizona and Texas. Hailstones the size of baseballs have ripped off roofs and leveled trees. These can do tremendous damage. But try to envision the damage inflicted by hailstones weighing a talent, between sixty and one hundred pounds.

These cataclysms of nature will, no doubt, bring great changes to our climate. The Bible says that the deserts will blossom like a rose, and there will be streams in the deserts and pools in the dry places (Isaiah 35:1, 6–7).

The curse will be removed. Botanists say that a thorn is an undeveloped leaf. A cactus could be extremely beautiful if every thorn became a leaf. God will restore the earth as He intended it to be when He first created man and placed him upon it. Jesus will establish His glorious kingdom on a rejuvenated garden-like earth.

I look forward to the day when we shall share together in God's kingdom. How beautiful that is going to be!

CHAPTER 17

COUNTERFEIT CHURCH

G od called Jeremiah to be a prophet to the nation Israel when he was just a teenager. God said,

I have this day set you over the nations and over the kingdoms, to root out, and to pull down, and to destroy, and to throw down, to build, and to plant (Jeremiah 1:10).

The condition of Israel had deteriorated so badly that, before God could build and plant, He first had to root out that which was left.

The condition of the world has become so serious and so bad that, before God can establish the eternal kingdom of righteousness and before He can build and plant, the systems of the world must first be rooted out, pulled down, and destroyed.

This is what we find in Revelation 17—the rooting out and the pulling down of that great religious system called "MYSTERY, BABYLON THE GREAT" (Rev. 17:5).

Cup of Abominations—We have some very difficult things to declare as we get into the destruction of this false religious system. They are difficult because we must be true to the Word of God, and we must recognize facts as they exist. Yet, in so doing, it is necessary to point the finger of accusation, as does the Scripture, at this false religious system.

It is important to realize that this is not a personal vendetta or a pronouncement against the people who, unfortunately, have been deceived by the system. It is important to realize that the Lord was talking to this same church in Revelation 2, the church of Thyatira. And He recognized that there were those within it who would overcome and be with Him in His kingdom.

It is tragic that the church's history is as ugly, dark, and bleak as it is. I have no defense for the history of the church.

A long time ago the church felt that it could do without the guiding hand of the Holy Spirit. It shook free from the governing power of the Spirit. The church said, "We can do it ourselves." Man attempted to build the church of Jesus Christ by himself—with elaborate structures, elaborate organizations, and elaborate rituals. All these things took away from the simplicity that is in Christ Jesus and made the approach to God very complex and ritualistic.

In reality, the approach to God is so simple and so easy. All you have to do is bow your head wherever you are and speak to the Father. You can have a close and intimate communication and fellowship with Him anywhere and anytime.

Through the development of religious systems, man set up all types of priorities and categories. With these came favoritism, the pandering to the rich and exclusive classes. Favoritism engenders the separation of people rather than bringing us all together as one body. A priesthood was established over the laity. He began to stand between God and man. Confession of sin was made to him. In Christ Jesus there is neither Jew nor Greek, free nor bond (Galatians 3:28). God looks upon us all alike and loves us all alike just as we are.

It is sad to study the history of the church, especially through the Middle and Dark Ages. We must confess that the Dark Ages resulted largely from the suppression by the church in trying to maintain tight and rigid control over people.

The early church suffered tremendous persecution by the Roman government. The Roman government martyred an estimated six million Christians in the first three hundred years of the church's existence. Being a Christian was a capital offense.

Then under Constantine the Great (AD 288–337) there was a great change. Constantine's mother was a Christian and had influence upon her son. When he came to the throne of Rome, he gave his edict of toleration of Christians. This meant that

Christians did not have to hail Caesar as their lord but could acknowledge Jesus Christ as their Lord.

Actually, it was an unfortunate day for the church. Suddenly, the church was thrust from a place of persecution into a place of power and authority. Then came the marriage of the church and state, and the state began to legislate the religious lives of the people. Men began to claim authority over both government and the church, seeking to combine the two.

However, they missed the mark. Righteousness can never be legislated. It is a matter of the heart.

We read with regret the history of the church during the Middle Ages when the office of the Pope was auctioned off to the highest bidder, and immorality and lewdness were practiced by the supposed Christian leaders. True spirituality had left the church.

The Great Compromise—In order to popularize Christianity, the church decided to take the pagan celebrations and "Christianize" them by giving them Christian names. It was a sad and tragic decision.

The church took on the pagan practice of Saturnalia. It was a Roman orgy holiday on December 25—a time for everybody to get drunk and give gifts to one another, light candles and build bonfires to help the poor old sun through the winter solstice.

The church proclaimed the 25th of December as the birthday of Jesus Christ and called it "Christmas." A mass was held for the birth of Christ on December 25 during the feast of Saturnalia.

Today we follow that same pagan practice. Christmas is becoming more paganized all the time in the world around us. It is now much as it was in Rome—a time for drunken parties and merriment, the giving of gifts, and riotous celebration.

The same juggling was true with the celebration of the coming of spring. Astarte was the goddess of perpetual life. Decorating eggs was part of the celebration because the egg was the symbol of perpetuated life. The church said, "We'll call this Easter and celebrate the resurrection of Jesus Christ from the dead."

The priesthood didn't exist in the early church but did exist in the Babylonian religion. The introduction of idols, the introduction of penance, even the worship and the rituals themselves, all had their origin in the Babylonian religion. These were gradually introduced and made part of the church. They were not existent in the early church but became a corrupt form of worship. The Lord calls them spiritual "fornication." This is actually the worship of God in unprescribed ways and manners. The Israelites sought to do this in the Old Testament. They were worshiping God after the ways of the pagans and heathens rather than after the way God had prescribed through Scripture.

During the period of the great Inquisitions, millions of true and faithful believers in Jesus Christ, who were looking for the simplicity and beauty of worshiping Him, were martyred. It is a fact of history. It's the black and dark history of the church that we hate to acknowledge. But you cannot deny the facts.

We do not seek to speak against our Christian brothers, and there are many beautiful Christian brothers and sisters today within the Catholic Church. I am so thankful for the revival that is taking place within the Catholic Church and I rejoice in what God is doing there. He is drawing out His overcomers. He is drawing them unto Himself. The spiritual revival within the Catholic Church today is unparalleled in its history.

In the Vatican, several thousand charismatic Catholics gathered together in St. Peter's for mass, worshiping God, and singing some of the choruses from Calvary Chapel. The Pope encouraged these believers to receive all the spiritual gifts and to become more fervent in their worship of God. Then he surprised them all by ending his speech with "Praise the Lord!" God is moving by His Spirit within that system. The true saints within that system will be raptured with the church. Those who remain to take it over and control it are false prophets. I've been praying for that for years and I'm thrilled to see it.

Nonetheless, the history is still there. That we cannot deny.

REVELATION 17:1-5

> And there came one of the seven angels which had the seven vials, and talked with me, saying unto me, Come, I will show you the judgment of the great whore that sits upon many waters (Rev. 17:1).

"Many waters" are the many nations. The "great whore" is the false church system which has gained such power and rules over so many nations.

> With whom the kings of the earth have committed fornication, and the inhabitants of the earth have been made drunk with the wine of her fornication. So he carried me away in the spirit into the wilderness: and I saw a woman sit upon a scarlet colored beast, full of names of blasphemy, having seven heads and ten horns (Rev. 17:2–3).

"Seven heads and ten horns" describes the Antichrist. In Revelation 13 the beast (Antichrist) came up out of the sea with seven heads and ten horns.

> And the woman was arrayed in purple and scarlet color, and decked with gold and precious stones and pearls, having a golden cup in her hand full of abominations and filthiness of her fornication: And upon her forehead was a name written, MYSTERY, BABYLON THE GREAT, THE MOTHER OF HARLOTS AND ABOMINATIONS OF THE EARTH (Rev. 17:4–5).

The identity of this church system was MYSTERY, BABYLON. I recommend the book, *The Two Babylons*, by Alexander Hislop to those students who desire to know more on this subject. Hislop makes the comparisons between the ancient Babylonian religion with this religious system that has ruled for so many years. The book is extremely enlightening, almost terrifyingly so.

REVELATION 17:6-9

> And I saw the woman drunken with the blood of the saints, and with the blood of the martyrs of Jesus: and

when I saw her, I wondered with great admiration. And the angel said unto me, Why did you marvel? I will tell you the mystery of the woman, and of the beast that carries her, which has the seven heads and ten horns (Rev. 17:6–7).

It seems that there will be a confederacy between this false church system and the Antichrist in the last days, which helps to put him into power. It is possible that this church system will be the false prophet that leads the world to worship the beast.

The beast that you saw was, and is not; and shall ascend out of the bottomless pit [*abyss*], and go into perdition: and they that dwell on the earth shall wonder, whose names were not written in the book of life from the foundation of the world, when they behold the beast that was, and is not, and yet is. And here is the mind which has wisdom. The seven heads are seven mountains, on which the woman sits (Rev. 17:8–9).

John identifies for us a specific city: "the seven heads are seven mountains." The city of Rome is built on seven hills. From ancient times, Rome has been known as "The City of Seven Hills."

REVELATION 17:10-11

And there are seven kings: five are fallen, and one is, and the other is not yet come; and when he comes, he must continue a short time. And the beast that was, and is not, even he is the eighth, and is of the seven, and goes into perdition (Rev. 17:10–11).

The identity of the "beast" is given for us in Revelation 17. He was, and he is not, and he shall ascend out of the *abyss*. The city of Rome is identified. John said there were seven kings, five of which are fallen. At the time that John wrote the Revelation, Domitian was the emperor of Rome. He was the sixth in order. After him, there was one further emperor. There is one more that is coming. He is the eighth, but he is of the seven.

It would seem that the Spirit is giving wisdom and understanding as to the identity of the Antichrist. The beast that

John saw "was, and is not; and shall ascend out of the *abyss*." Then he goes into perdition or destruction.

The Nero File—The fifth emperor of the Roman empire was Caesar Nero. He was known by the early church as "The Beast." He is a man of interesting history, for there was a dramatic change in his life. When he first ascended as the Roman emperor he seemed to be a fairly levelheaded fellow. He started many beneficial building projects for the people. He actually started the Corinthian canal; however, that project was never completed by him.

Suddenly, a dramatic change came in Nero's life and he became as another person. It is interesting that this drastic change occurred shortly after Paul stood before him in defense of the Gospel. When Paul the apostle was getting the run-around in Caesarea, he appealed unto Caesar. Festus, the Roman governor, said, "Have you appealed unto Caesar? Unto Caesar you shall go" (Acts 25:12). Paul was sent to Rome so that he might appeal his case before Caesar Nero.

Now, I have no doubt that, when Paul appealed his case before Nero, he made every endeavor to convert the emperor to a belief in Jesus Christ. That was Paul's method. As he defended himself before the Jews, and as he defended himself before Felix and before Agrippa, he used it as an opportunity to lead these men to Jesus Christ. I am certain that he laid a witness on Nero the likes of which he had never heard. When Paul was through with the defense, Nero knew exactly where he stood in relation to the Lord Jesus Christ.

Nero let Paul go, but shortly afterwards the emperor seemed to turn suddenly mad. I believe that, in rejecting the message that Paul gave him, Nero actually opened the door to Satan within his life and became demon-possessed.

Nero set Rome ablaze and had an insane glee as the city burned. He used it as an occasion to blame the Christians and start a bloody movement against them. He would cover the Christians with tar and set them afire in his garden. Shrieking and in the nude, he'd drive his chariot in the midst of the burning bodies of

Christians. He had Paul arrested again, brought back to Rome, and beheaded. He brought Peter to Rome and crucified him upside down.

At the time that the Lord was speaking to John in the Revelation, Nero had already died. He was, but he is not. But he shall ascend out of the *abyss*. I believe that the same demon that possessed Caesar Nero will possess the Antichrist who will come to reign over the earth. Thus, all the marks of Caesar Nero will be upon this man of sin.

Revelation 13 said, "Here is wisdom. Let him who has understanding count the number of the beast: for it is the number of a man" (Rev. 13:18).

In Greek and Hebrew the letters have numeric equivalents. In Hebrew the letters of the name "Caesar Nero" total to 666. I do believe that the demon which possessed Caesar Nero will possess the Antichrist; in a sense, he will be a reincarnation, as the same demon will come out of the *abyss*. Some of the same deeds and actions seen in Nero will be manifested by this man of sin which is to come.

REVELATION 17:12-13

"And the ten horns which you saw are ten kings" (Rev. 17:12). These are the ten kings or the confederation of ten European nations that will comprise the final world power.

King Nebuchadnezzar had a vision in which he saw an image with a head of gold, the arms and breast of silver, the stomach of brass, the legs of iron, and the feet of iron and clay with ten toes (Daniel 2:31–45). He was looking at that great image until he saw a rock that was not cut with hands come from the mountains. This rock struck the great image in the feet so that the whole figure fell. The rock grew into a great mountain that covered the earth, and there was no end of that kingdom.

When Daniel interpreted the dream of Nebuchadnezzar, he said, "Nebuchadnezzar, the Lord of heaven has showed you the governments that shall rule the world. You, Nebuchadnezzar, are the head of gold. But your kingdom is to be replaced by the Medo-Persian empire, the arms and the shoulders of silver. That government in turn will be replaced by the Grecian government, the stomach of brass; which will be replaced by the Roman government, the legs of iron. But the final government of man will be a mixture of iron and clay, the feet with ten toes." It is during the time of this kingdom that the rock comes from the mountain. It destroys the earthly governments of man and establishes the kingdom that shall never end.

It is clear that Nebuchadnezzar's dream has been fulfilled in history. God is setting the whole stage for the final scene.

> The ten horns which you saw are ten kings, which have received no kingdom as yet; but they receive power as kings one hour with the beast. These have one mind, and shall give their power and strength unto the beast (Rev. 17:12–13).

The European Community now formed finds it's weakness in the clay. The disputes that arise are over the multi-rule, each nation naturally looking for it's own benefit. To ultimately gain the full potential of the union, they must give one man decisive power to lead this flock of nations. They'll give their power unto one man, the Antichrist.

REVELATION 17:14-18

> These shall make war with the Lamb, and the Lamb shall overcome them: for he is Lord of lords, and King of kings: and they that are with him are called, and chosen, and faithful (Rev. 17:14).

Here are three qualities of those who are with Jesus. They are called, ordained, and faithful. Jesus said that you have not chosen Him, but He has chosen you, and ordained you, that you should be His disciples (John 15:16).

> And he said unto me, The waters which you saw where the whore sits, are peoples, and multitudes, and nations, and

tongues. And the ten horns which you saw upon the beast, these shall hate the whore, and shall make her desolate and naked, and shall eat her flesh, and burn her with fire. For God has put in their hearts to fulfill His will, and to agree, and give their kingdom unto the beast, until the words of God shall be fulfilled. And the woman which you saw is that great city, which reigns over the kings of the earth (Rev. 17:15–18).

The city of Rome, which reigned over the kings of the earth at the time that John wrote, shall rise again to a place of prominence in a federation of ten nations. Thus, we see the final judgment of God upon both that great city and the religious system that arose out of that city.

CHAPTER 18

BANKRUPTCY

(G) od said, Love not the world, neither the things that are in the world. If any man loves the world, the love of the Father is not in him (1 John 2:15). The Lord also said, Come out from among them, and be separate, and touch not the unclean thing; and I... will be a Father unto you, and you shall be My sons and daughters (2 Corinthians 6:17–18).

The "world" in the Scriptures is represented in three aspects: political, religious, and commercial. In Revelation the political world system is headed by the Antichrist while the world religious system is headed by the Great Whore, THE MOTHER OF HARLOTS, THE MYSTERY, BABYLON. The Whore is that great ecclesiastical system of religion without real life in Christ. Through MYSTERY, BABYLON the false prophet leads the world to worship the Antichrist.

Finally, the commercial world is represented by commercial Babylon.

Babylon was the first great world empire that man established after the flood. Shem, the son of Noah, settled in the Babylonian plains where the world empires began. Babylon was a commercial and a religious empire representing Satan's work in the world. It represents, in a collective sense, the world that the Bible warns Christians against.

There's a big push on today for a world monetary system, a world government, and a world religion—and these things shall be. The world government will be headed by the Antichrist and, as the political and commercial interests blend together, the Antichrist will gain control of the world's monetary system. No man will be able to buy or sell without the mark of the Antichrist.

In Revelation 17 we saw the destruction of the world's religious system—MYSTERY, BABYLON. In Revelation 18 we come to the destruction of commercial Babylon. Though religious Babylon was headquartered in Rome, the Scripture leaves the location of commercial Babylon a mystery.

Many Bible expositors believe that the ancient city of Babylon will actually be rebuilt, in order to be destroyed as prophesied in Revelation 18. They believe that ancient Babylon will become the commercial center of the world once again. They say that the prophecies about Babylon never to rise again (Isaiah 13:19–22; Jeremiah 51) have not been literally and completely fulfilled; thus, in order for the absolute fulfillment of prophecy, the ancient city of Babylon must be rebuilt on the River Euphrates.

Personally, as I read its history and look at the ruins of Babylon today, I believe that the prophecies of Isaiah and Jeremiah have been sufficiently fulfilled concerning that ancient city, and I don't think that Babylon must be rebuilt for this prophecy in Revelation 18 to be fulfilled.

However, the sudden shift of the world's wealth to the Middle East is a very interesting development. With the billions of dollars pouring in through the oil wealth, the Arabs may possibly decide to build one colossal city, ancient Babylon, again.

There are those who *insist* that Babylon has to be rebuilt. I do not believe that it *has* to be rebuilt. As Babylon was religiously represented by the city of Rome, so commercial Babylon could be represented by any great commercial center of the world. Babylon is evidently a seaport town, and all the commercial interests in the world will be centered in this great city. It may be New York; it may be another major seaport already in existence; or it may be that Babylon will be rebuilt.

Get Those Bucks!—We pride ourselves in free enterprise and in our tremendous power to purchase and to possess goods and services. But there is a certain evil that is inherent within commercialism—the exploitation of people.

Today, the world is suffering from the gigantic commercial interests which exploit the common people, you and me. In past times, a sharp division always existed between the political and commercial interests. The kings ruled separately from the merchant men. But today there has been a marriage of the commercial interests with the political powers. Big money rules. Wars are designed and plotted for the profits of the large commercial interests. Man is exploited today by commercialism. We're the victims of this satanic system.

God is going to bring an end to this godless commercial system that attains such tremendous power in the final period of man's history.

The word *babel* means "confused." Today, man's religion has become confused; man's politics have become confused; and the commercial economics of man have certainly become confused. In Revelation 18 we read of the destruction to come after these things—the death of the great Babylonian commercial system.

REVELATION 18:1-5

After these things I saw another angel come down from heaven, having great power; and the earth was lightened with his glory (Rev. 18:1).

Angels must be extremely interesting beings. This one coming down from heaven is a powerful angel because the earth lights up with his glory.

And he cried mightily with a strong voice, saying, Babylon the great is fallen, is fallen, and is become the habitation of devils, and the hold of every foul spirit, and a cage of every unclean and hateful bird. For all nations have drunk of the wine of the wrath of her fornication, and the kings of the earth have committed fornication with her, and the merchants of the earth are waxed rich through the abundance of her delicacies (Rev. 18:2–3).

The great commercial system, which has been married to the politics of the world and has become the habitation of the devils and every foul spirit, is falling.

It's interesting that, in New York City, Wall Street represents the commercial interests, Park Avenue represents the church section, and the whole system represents "The World." In the opening of Revelation 18 the nations have drunk of the wine of the wrath of Babylon's fornication, the kings of the earth commit fornication with her, and the merchants of the earth are waxed rich through the abundance of her delicacies.

As we look at this monolithic commercial system which has controlled the world and today controls our lives, we realize that the policies of nations are formed by and for commercial interests' sake. More and more of our lives are being manipulated by schemes such as planned shortages so that these forces can gain more money. Through more money they gain more power. We are the victims, and we are helpless to do anything about it.

These men play chess with the lives of the people of the world. Apparently, they do not have to answer to any man. They seem to sit as a queen in the world, and no one can touch them. Yet, God says that their judgment will be double that which they have done (v. 6).

And I heard another voice from heaven, saying, Come out of her, my people, that you be not partakers of her sins, and that you receive not of her plagues. For her sins have reached unto heaven, and God has remembered her iniquities (Rev. 18:4–5).

God is calling His people, the nation of the Jews, to come out of this commercial system.

Many times people have misinterpreted this particular Scripture. They say God is referring to religious Babylon. This isn't religious Babylon at all. In context, it's commercial Babylon.

The Local Church, directed by the late Witness Lee, calls all other churches "Babylon." They quote this Scripture often, "Come out of her, my people." Those who join the Local Church say that they've been freed from Babylon. That is a misapplication.

God is calling His people, the Jews, to come out of Babylon because of the plagues that she shall now receive.

REVELATION 18:6-10

Reward her even as she rewarded you, and double unto her double according to her works: in the cup which she has filled fill to her double. How much she has glorified herself, and lived deliciously, so much torment and sorrow give her: for she says in her heart, I sit a queen, and am no widow, and shall see no sorrow. Therefore shall her plagues come in one day, death, and mourning, and famine; and she shall be utterly burned with fire: for strong is the Lord God who judges her. And the kings of the earth, who have committed fornication and lived deliciously with her, shall bewail her, and lament for her, when they shall see the smoke of her burning, standing afar off for the fear of her torment saying, Alas, alas that great city Babylon, that mighty city! For in one hour is your judgment come (Rev. 18:6-10).

The destruction of Babylon will be swift. In one hour she will be wiped out. The smoke of her destruction will arise.

It would appear to me that the great city of Babylon, whatever city is the center of world commerce at that time, will be wiped out with a nuclear blast. The "fear of her torment" could actually be the fear of radioactivity in the area. The Scripture makes mention twice that people are standing afar off to bewail for fear of the torment (vv. 10, 15). We see this great commercial system brought to an end in one hour, and the fear of those who see it and who even dread to approach it.

REVELATION 18:11-14A

"And the merchants of the earth shall weep and mourn over her; for no man buys their merchandise any more" (Rev. 18:11).

James said, "Go to now, you rich men, weep and howl for your miseries that shall come upon you... Your gold and silver is cankered" (James 5:1, 3). This is the fall of commercialism. For those who have exploited the desires of man and have lived off and gouged others so that they themselves might live delicately, the day of judgment is coming. They will be brought down.

> The merchandise of gold, silver, precious stones, of pearls, fine linen, purple, silk, scarlet, all thyne wood, and all manner vessels of ivory, all manner vessels of most precious wood, brass, iron, marble, cinnamon, odors, ointments, frankincense, wine, oil, fine flour, wheat, beasts sheep, horses, chariots, slaves, and souls of men (Rev. 18:12–13).

Notice that the corrupt merchandising is not in necessities but in luxuries. The commercial interests have created and developed the market for luxury items. This is how they gain control over men's lives. The word *slaves* literally means "bodies." People sell their bodies and their souls so they can live in the luxuries of these possessions.

"And the fruits that your soul lusted after are departed from you" (Rev. 18:14a).

The Good Life—The advertising interests have created needs through their clever advertising schemes. They make you feel that you're not a complete or total person unless you use that particular deodorant. You can't truly obtain full manhood unless you use that particular cologne. The whole system is based upon creating a fictitious need in your mind so that you're not purchasing out of absolute necessity but just to be "in."

People who fall for these gimmicks have made themselves slaves to these great commercial interests. A good portion of their paycheck every week has to go to pay off the big-screen television, new car, or latest extravagance. Man has become a victim. We find ourselves helplessly and hopelessly over our heads in debt and unable to afford the real needs of life, because we've been enticed with the luxuries, the ease, and the soft things of life.

Jesus said that a man's life consists not in the abundance of the things which he possesses (Luke 12:15). Paul the apostle said, "Having food and raiment let us be therewith content... Godliness with contentment is great gain" (1 Timothy 6:8, 6). So many people have to buy a new wardrobe, not because their old clothes are worn out, but because they're just not in fashion this year. God would have you freed from slavery to the latest fashions and the grip of this damnable, hellish, devilish commercial system that is about to be judged.

Jesus Christ can set you free from the whole commercial system.

Liberated—God in His love has set men free from this slavery. The glorious reality about coming to Jesus Christ and acknowledging Him as your King is that you're no longer a slave to the world systems. Let them try to entice me to go into debt for some crummy thing. Not on your life! I don't have to have it! Praise the Lord, I'm happy without it. You don't have to have all that garbage to make you happy, because you can have it all and be miserable. But you can have nothing and be very happy if you have Jesus Christ. That's where real happiness and contentment lie. A material possession really doesn't make any difference. If you have it, praise the Lord! If you don't have it, praise the Lord!

That's a glorious aspect of being a Christian. You're no longer a slave to these things. You've been set free by Jesus Christ, and that's so beautiful. Paul said, "I know how to have, I know how to be in need, I know how to be abased, and I know how to abound. I have learned to be content in whatever state I'm in" (Philippians 4:11-12). That is a great secret—to be content because I have God wherever I am. My life belongs to Him and, as far as this world is concerned, I'm just a pilgrim. This isn't my home, thank God!

Other people don't understand. They get uptight because I'm not playing their little games or dancing to their tunes. They can get uptight all they want. It doesn't bother me a bit because I know that I'm just a pilgrim and a stranger. I'm looking for the kingdom of God. I'm waiting for that day very soon when I'll pass from this life and enter into that eternal kingdom.

In one way I really rejoiced in the hippie movement. When the young people started rebelling against the materialistic society, the great commercial interests became very upset. Kids were no longer bugging their dads for new Corvettes. They would ride a bike or walk or hitchhike. They didn't even care if they had a car—an old broken-down van was fine.

Of course, commercialism regrouped and re-planned. The advertisers started to create new demands, new interests, and new desires. And, finally, they got things back under their control. But, for a while, the kids really had them shook. I sat back laughing. "Kids, that's right! You don't need all those things. They won't bring you happiness or joy. They won't bring you peace or contentment." And, as I saw them going back to nature, I knew that they were closer to the real answer. For the closer you get to nature, then the closer you get to God, if you look at nature in a rational way.

REVELATION 18:14B-19

> And all things which were dainty and goodly are departed from you, and you shall find them no more at all. The merchants of these things, which were made rich by her, shall stand afar off for the fear of her torment, weeping and wailing (Rev. 18:14,15).

What a tragic sight when God's judgment falls! Merchants, kings, and seamen are all standing around, weeping and wailing.

> Saying, Alas, alas that great city, that was clothed in fine linen, and purple, and scarlet, and decked with gold, and precious stones, and pearls! For in one hour so great riches is come to nothing. And every shipmaster, and all the company in ships, and sailors, and as many as trade by sea, stood afar off, and cried when they saw the smoke of her burning, saying, What city is like unto this great city! And they cast dust on their heads, and cried, weeping and wailing, saying, Alas, alas that great city, wherein were made rich all that had ships in the sea by reason of her costliness! For in one hour is she made desolate (Rev. 18:16–19).

These facts are emphasized over and over again: the destruction came in one hour; those who see it are afraid to approach it; there is great weeping and crying and lamenting by those who had profited and gained by this vast commercial system, Babylon.

REVELATION 18:20-24

While all this destruction is happening on earth, there is an entirely different scene going on in heaven.

Rejoice over her, you heaven, and you holy apostles and prophets; for God has avenged you on her. And a mighty angel took up a stone like a great millstone, and cast it into the sea, saying, Thus with violence shall that great city Babylon be thrown down, and shall be found no more at all. And the voice of harpers, and musicians, and of pipers, and trumpeters, shall be heard no more at all in you; and no craftsman, of whatsoever craft he be, shall be found any more in you; and the sound of a millstone shall be heard no more at all in you; and the light of a candle shall shine no more at all in you; and the voice of the bridegroom and of the bride shall be heard no more at all in you: for your merchants were the great men of the earth; for by your sorceries were all nations deceived (Rev. 18:20–23).

As I mentioned before, I think this deception refers to advertisements.

"In her was found the blood of prophets, and of saints, and of all that were slain upon the earth" (Rev. 18:24).

Whether or not this is a sequel to religious Babylon and stands for the destruction of Rome, I do not know. There may be another city that represents the commercial Babylon of the world, or Babylon may actually be rebuilt on the River Euphrates. I am open on this particular issue.

The Other Side—Next, we enter into a new phase of Revelation. The kingdom of God will replace the corrupt and polluted world system that has brought the earth such misery, woe, and suffering.

In the kingdom age, the Lord said, "Ho, every one that thirsts, come to the waters, and he that has no money; come, buy, and eat" (Isaiah 55:1). Those things that we have during the kingdom age will be free and available to all men. There will be no commerce in the kingdom age. There will be a total sharing of all things without the exploitation of man.

When communism came along, its ideal was to bring everybody by force to a common level. The Lord's plan is to bring everybody by love to a common level.

Love will be the common denominator among men. We will want to share all that we have with one another. There will be no poor, no destitute, no needy. There will be that complete sharing together of God's glorious resources during the kingdom age.

I'll be glad when this planet gets to the other side of the seven years of great tribulation. It's a rough road all the way. How glorious to come into the kingdom age of God in Revelation 19!

CHAPTER 19
JESUS COMES AGAIN

REVELATION 19:1-4

A nd after these things I heard a great voice of much people in heaven, saying, Alleluia; Salvation, and glory, and honor, and power, unto the Lord our God: for true and righteous are his judgments: for He has judged the great whore, which did corrupt the earth with her fornication, and has avenged the blood of his servants at her hand. And again they said, Alleluia. And her [the great whore who was punished] smoke rose up for ever and ever. And the four and twenty elders and the four living creatures fell down and worshiped God that sat on the throne, saying, Amen; Alleluia (Rev. 19:1–4).

Here the church is in heaven, worshiping and praising the Lord. Salvation, glory, honor and power to the Lord our God! We're declaring the righteousness of the judgments of God.

Today, we hear so many people questioning the judgments of God. "Is God fair when He judges?" However, when we see the final judgment of God upon the earth, there will be that acknowledgment of the fairness and the righteousness of God in His judgments.

The justice of man's system is quite corrupt. We can't say, "True and righteous are the judgments of the courts of the United States." They're not always so true and not always so righteous. The problem is, how can we really know all the facts? We get conflicting testimonies. But when God judges, He knows all the details and all the motives. He will be true and righteous.

REVELATION 19:5-8

> And a voice came out of the throne, saying, Praise our
> God, all you His servants, and you that fear Him, both
> small and great. And I heard as it were the voice of a great
> multitude, and as the voice of many waters, and as the
> voice of mighty thunderings, saying, Alleluia: for the Lord
> God omnipotent reigns (Rev. 19:5–6).

At this present time, it doesn't seem that God really reigns.
Many times we feel that God has vacated the throne—as He's
allowed calamities to come upon the earth. We see the fruit and the
results of man's rebellion against God all around us. In times of
trouble we wonder, "God, where are you?"

But the day of judgment is coming, and God will bring to
naught every opposing force. Then there will be that glorious shout
in heaven by all the church of God. It will sound like thunder
rumbling in the distance. It will sound like a mighty waterfall as we
declare, "Alleluia! For the Lord God omnipotent reigns."

Marriage Supper of the Lamb—

> Let us be glad and rejoice, and give honor to Him: for the
> marriage of the Lamb is come, and His wife has made
> herself ready (Rev. 19:7).

The Lamb, of course, is Jesus Christ. The wife is the church.
Now the time has come for the glorious uniting of Jesus with His
church. The marriage of the Lamb has come and the wife has made
herself ready.

> And to her was granted that she should be arrayed in fine
> linen, clean and white: for the fine linen is the
> righteousness of the saints (Rev. 19:8).

The righteousness of the saints is actually the righteousness
which is imputed to us through our faith in Jesus Christ. The
righteousness of the saints is not achieved by keeping rules and
regulations and ordinances. God has imputed righteousness to you
because of your faith in Jesus Christ.

REVELATION 19:9-10

> And he says unto me, Write, Blessed are they which are called unto the marriage supper of the Lamb. And he says unto me, These are the true sayings of God. And I fell at his feet to worship him. And he said unto me, See that you do not do that: I am your fellow servant, and of your brethren that have the testimony of Jesus: worship God: for the testimony of Jesus is the spirit of prophecy (Rev. 19:9–10).

Revelation 1 began, "The Revelation of Jesus Christ, which God gave unto him, to show unto his servants things which must shortly come to pass; and He sent and signified it by His angel unto His servant John." In much of the Revelation the angel is speaking unto John. John views the glorious scene of the church in heaven, clothed in the righteousness of Christ and ready to be received by Him, and he is just overwhelmed. As the angel reveals these glorious truths and wonders and says to John, "These are the true sayings of God." The Bible speaks of the sure word of prophesy in 2 Peter 1:19. When Daniel interpreted Nebuchadnezzar's dream he declared, "The dream is certain, and the interpretation is sure." God speaks of the future, then He attests to the accuracy of what he has spoken. John then falls on his face to worship the angel who responds. "Stand up! I'm just like you are. I'm a fellow servant. Worship God." Then he declares, "For the testimony of Jesus is the spirit of prophecy."

All prophecy centers around Jesus Christ. The entire Old Testament concerns Jesus Christ. Jesus said, "Search the Scriptures; for in them you think you have eternal life: and they are they which testify of me" (John 5:39). He is the heart and the soul of the Scriptures. He said, "Lo, I come (in the volume of the book it is written of me,) to do Your will, O God" (Hebrews 10:7). The spirit of prophecy is the testimony of Jesus Christ.

Whenever the Spirit of God is speaking in prophecy today, He is exalting Jesus Christ. The ministry and the work of the Holy Spirit is to exalt the Lord, not any man. At a true moving of God's Spirit, hearts and lives of people are drawn to Jesus Christ.

REVELATION 19:11-15

Maranatha! Fulfilled—"And I saw heaven opened, and behold
a white horse; and he that sat upon him was called Faithful and
True" (Rev. 19:11). In Revelation 1:5 and also in His message to
the church of Laodicea (Rev. 3:14), Jesus is described as the faithful
and true witness of God.

"And in righteousness He judges and makes war" (Rev. 19:11).
There is such a thing as a righteous war—and the Lord will wage
it.

> His eyes were as a flame of fire, and on His head were
> many crowns; and He had a name written, that no man
> knew, but He Himself. And He was clothed with a vesture
> dipped in blood: and His name is called The Word of God
> (Rev. 19:12–13).

> In the beginning was the Word, and the Word was with
> God, and the Word was God. The same was in the
> beginning with God. All things were made by Him; and
> without Him was not any thing made that was made. In
> Him was life; and the life was the light of men. And the
> light shines in darkness; and the darkness comprehended it
> not... He came unto His own, and His own received Him
> not. But as many as received Him, to them gave He power
> to become the sons of God, even to them that believe on
> His name: Which were born, not of blood, nor of the will
> of the flesh, nor of the will of man, but of God. And the
> Word was made flesh, and dwelt among us, (and we
> beheld his glory, the glory as of the only begotten of the
> Father,) full of grace and truth" (John 1:1–5, 11–14).

As Jesus comes back again riding on the white horse to reign
upon the earth and establish God's kingdom, He has on His crown
the name written "The Word of God."

Praise the Lord—here's where *you* come in! "The armies which
were in heaven followed Him upon white horses, clothed in fine
linen, white and clean" (Rev. 19:14). This is what you were robed
in when you made yourself ready for the marriage supper of the
Lamb. Now you return with Jesus Christ as He comes back to

establish His reign upon the earth. "When Christ, who is our life, shall appear, then shall you also appear with Him in glory," the Bible tells us (Colossians 3:4).

> And out of His mouth goes a sharp sword, that with it He should smite the nations: and He shall rule them with a rod of iron: and He treads the winepress of the fierceness and wrath of Almighty God (Rev. 19:15).

The Word of God is alive and powerful and sharper than any two-edged sword (Hebrews 4:12). The Word that goes forth out of the mouth of Christ is powerful. "And God said, Let there be light: and there was light" (Genesis 1:3). The power in the Word of God!

"And He shall rule them with a rod of iron." The word *rule* in the Greek is the word "shepherd." "He will shepherd them." This speaks of the nature of the rule He will have. Jesus said, "I am the good shepherd... and I lay down My life for the sheep" (John 10:14–15). David said, "The LORD is my shepherd; I shall not want. He makes me to lie down in green pastures: He leads me beside the still waters" (Psalm 23:12). Jesus will shepherd them with the rod. Shepherds have always had rods. Instead of a wooden rod, His will be a rod of iron.

REVELATION 19:16-21

> And He has on His vesture and on His thigh a name written, KING OF KINGS, AND LORD OF LORDS. And I saw an angel standing in the sun; and he cried with a loud voice, saying to all the fowls that fly in the midst of heaven, Come and gather yourselves together unto the supper of the great God; that you may eat the flesh of kings, and the flesh of captains, and the flesh of mighty men, and the flesh of horses, and of them that sit on them, and the flesh of all men, both free and bond, both small and great. And I saw the beast, and the kings of the earth, and their armies, gathered together to make war against Him that sat on the horse, and against His army (Rev. 19:16–19).

Here we see the culmination of the Battle of Armageddon where the evil spirits have gone forth from the Antichrist, the false prophet, and Satan to gather the kings of the earth into the valley of Megiddo for the great battle against God. Jesus Christ will just speak the Word and they will be destroyed.

When this conflict is in full swing, Jesus Christ will come again with His church and all the saints.

The beast has tremendous power, so much so that people will say, "Who is able to make war against the beast, or to stand against him?" (Rev. 13:4). Only the King of Kings and the Lord of Lords has the power to do so. With the brightness of the Lord's coming, the Antichrist will be destroyed (2 Thessalonians 2:8).

And the beast was taken, and with him the false prophet that wrought miracles before him, with which he deceived them that had received the mark of the beast, and them that worshiped his image. These both were cast alive into the lake of fire burning with brimstone (Rev. 19:20).

The description is of the place the Scripture calls Gehenna, the lake of fire burning with brimstone.

And the remnant [the armies and others that followed the Antichrist] were slain with the sword of Him that sat upon the horse, which sword proceeded out of His mouth: and all the fowls were filled with their flesh (Rev. 19:21).

With the Word, Jesus will put an end to man's rebellion against God.

CHAPTER 20

THE PERFECT GOVERNMENT

REVELATION 20:1-3

nd I saw an angel come down from heaven, having the key of the bottomless pit and a great chain in his hand (Rev. 20:1).

The "bottomless pit" in the Greek is the *abyss*. In Revelation 9, Satan, who was the angel of the *abyss*, opened it and loosed the demon hordes. They spread throughout the world, bringing great destruction, pain, torment, and death.

> He laid hold on the dragon, that old serpent, which is the Devil, and Satan, and bound him a thousand years, and cast him into the *abyss*, and shut him up, and set a seal upon him, that he should deceive the nations no more, till the thousand years should be fulfilled: and after that he must be loosed a little season (Rev. 20:2–3).

Let no man deceive you that the day of the Lord has already come and that we are in the kingdom age. Here we read that in the kingdom age Satan will actually be bound by a great chain and cast into the *abyss*. This hasn't happened yet. Satan is still able to exercise great wrath and power over the earth. The earth today is not under the authority of Jesus Christ. When Jesus Christ shall come to reign, the angel will take this great chain and bind Satan, casting him into the *abyss*.

Satan will be bound and kept, sealed and chained in the *abyss* for one thousand years. Then, he shall be loosed for a short season. Now, if God once has him chained, why would He ever loose him again? One of the big questions is, "Why did God ever let Satan go free? If God is finally going to do him in, why didn't He do it a long time ago and save us all this misery?"

The reason is that God wants you to love Him freely. You see, God could have made everything good. Then there would be no evil and, thus, no alternative. God wants to know that you truly love Him and serve Him by your own choice.

It's like a problem you may have if you are very beautiful. You never know whether a person loves you because you look beautiful or because you are you. That's also one of the problems of being extremely rich. You don't know whether they love you or whether they have visions of spending your riches. How would you know whether they really love you?

God wants to know that you really love Him. Thus, He gave you a free will and an alternate choice. He has left Satan free to exploit the alternate choice so that when you come to God and worship Him, praise Him, and express your love to Him, He knows that it is real and genuine. He receives glory through your praise because He knows it's from your heart. Sometimes that's very hard to do because Satan is always there to keep you from truly loving God. Thus, God receives true glory from our sincere praise and trust in Him.

In Training—Jesus told an interesting parable of a lord who entrusted his goods to his servants while he went away into a far country. To one servant he gave five talents, to another he gave two, and to another he gave one. When the lord returned, the servant who had received the five talents brought him ten talents. He said, "Here, lord. You gave me five and now I've doubled them." The lord replied, "Well done, you good and faithful servant. You have been faithful over a few things, I will make you ruler over many things: enter into the joy of your lord."

The servant to whom he gave two talents said, "I have used them, and I've traded with them, and now I have four talents." The lord again said, "Well done, you good and faithful servant. You have been faithful over a few things, I will make you ruler over many things: enter into the joy of your lord."

The servant with the one talent buried it and said, "Lord, I just buried it. Here it is. It's all neat and I haven't touched it. I know you're an austere man. I know that you reap where you haven't sowed." The lord replied, "Yes, you knew all that, so you're judged by your own knowledge" (Matthew 25:14–30).

Jesus' parable points out that, when we enter with Him into the kingdom age, there will be varying degrees of responsibility given to us according to our faithfulness with what He is now entrusting to us. At that time we will be apportioned an area of the world. If we're diligent now with what God has placed in our hands and use it for Him, then we'll have a place of greater responsibility in the kingdom age. (This fact is especially brought out in Luke 19:12–17.)

If we are lazy now and do not use what God has given us, it's possible we'll be lazy then. Actually, the lord took away the one talent from the lax servant and gave it to him who had ten.

When we return with Jesus, we are coming back to an earth that will be restored to beauty once again by God. It will be a whole new system. As far as economics, we won't have money as we know it today. God is going to provide everything. The earth will again produce abundantly. With Satan bound and out of the way, man won't be ruled by greed anymore.

There will be no war. There will be no suffering, no disease, no sickness, no hardships, and no hatred. We will live together in peace and love in God's glorious kingdom. I can hardly wait!

From Rags to Riches—We, the Christians, will be in our new glorified bodies when we come back with Christ to reign with Him upon the earth. Our new bodies will have many advantages over our old corruptible bodies which are rapidly decaying.

Whenever you're dealing with matter, you're dealing with a temporary substance. The whole material universe is slowly going to pieces. Sir John Herschel, the great scientist, said that the universe is like a gigantic clock that has been wound up and is slowly running down. The sun is losing 1.2 million tons of mass every second. It can't last more than ten billion years at that rate. The laws of thermodynamics are taking their toll and everything is gradually degrading and going down, down, down.

God made our new bodies in a new manner. They're made from heavenly elements. You'll be able to walk right through a material wall. It's as if you were to shine a flashlight at a one-foot thick piece of glass, the light would shine through to the other side. Similarly, after Jesus was resurrected from the dead, He evidently passed through the walls into the room where the disciples were gathered (John 20:26). All the doors were locked and, suddenly, Christ appeared in their midst and began talking to them.

Our new bodies will probably be made of a different molecular structure than the material universe. As far as we know, in this material universe everything is made up of three building blocks: protons, electrons, and neutrons. God has created such an infinite variety from these three components by combining them in different ways. How do we know that God doesn't have other building blocks? Why should God limit Himself to three? God made our earthly bodies out of these three building blocks and God has another body waiting for us. He said that as we have borne the image of the earthy, so shall we bear the image of the heavenly (1 Corinthians 15:49). Those building blocks God used to create heaven are the building blocks He has used to make your new body.

There will be no tiring effects on our new bodies and we'll never need any sleep. Very likely, we'll be able to move around with the great ease and speed that the angels do. Just think of a place and you'll be there!

A New Role—The Pharisees tried to trap Jesus one time by making up a silly situation. Under the Jewish law, when you married a woman and then died before bearing any children, your brother had to marry the widow so she could bear children for your name. The Pharisees made up a situation in which a woman married seven times and, each time she married, her husband died before she had any children. Seven brothers married her and all seven died without fathering any children.

"In the resurrection," they said to Jesus, "whose wife shall she be of the seven?" They pictured all seven husbands fighting over her in the resurrection. Jesus answered, "You do err, not knowing the Scriptures… For in the resurrection," He said, "they neither marry, nor are given in marriage, but are as the angels of God in heaven" (Matthew 22:23–30).

People talk about marriage as an eternal state. It really isn't. Then what's the purpose of marriage? God has designed marriage as a family unit in which to raise children. The best environment in the world for children is in a family setting.

In the kingdom age we'll be as the angels who neither marry nor are given in marriage. Then what relationship will we have with one another? It will be a beautiful, deep, and glorious relationship, but it won't be a marriage-type relationship. Now, God didn't say we would be sexless. I don't know if the angels are or not. Generally, the angels in the Bible appear as men, but I don't know whether that proves anything. All we know is that we'll be as the angels who neither marry nor are given in marriage.

Scripture says that in Christ there is neither Jew, barbarian, bond or free. Also there is neither male nor female, but Christ is all and in all (Colossians 3:11). You won't need women's lib for equal rights. We're all one in Christ Jesus, and we certainly shall be so in the kingdom age.

REVELATION 20:4

> And I saw thrones, and they sat upon them, and judgment was given unto them: and I saw the souls of them that were beheaded for the witness of Jesus, and for the Word of God, and which had not worshiped the beast, neither his image, neither had received his mark upon their foreheads, or in their hands; and they lived and reigned with Christ a thousand years (Rev. 20:4).

Who will be upon the earth during the kingdom age? First, the church will be coming back with Jesus Christ. Second, those martyred during the Tribulation period, who did not take the mark of the beast and were slain for their testimony, will come back to rule and reign with Jesus for the thousand years. I believe that the Old Testament saints will also be coming back.

Who else will be upon the earth? Those few who are able to survive the great tribulation without taking the mark of the beast or worshiping his image.

When Christ comes again He will judge the world in righteousness; and those who have taken the mark of the beast, worshiped the image, and have fallen prey to his system will be wiped out at that time. They will not be able to enter into the kingdom age and live on the earth during the reign of Christ.

How many people will be able to survive the great tribulation? That is only a matter of speculation. There is one Scripture that hints one out of three Jews will survive (Zechariah 13:8–9). There will be some who do survive, but not many.

Just a word of advice to certain people. Maybe you don't want to accept Jesus Christ and would rather go the hard way. You'll have to find some means of surviving for seven years without depending on this corrupt society. This society will be totally taken over. The economy will be taken over by the Antichrist. No one will be able to buy or sell except he has his mark. If you take the mark, you are lost forever.

The best plan is probably to take off for the jungles of Mexico and learn how to live off the land. Just do your best to survive down there. I would also suggest the remote areas of Oregon but I don't know how you'd survive the winters there.

There is a great jungle area in Mexico near the Guatemalan border. No, I don't plan to be there. I'm just giving a tip for those people who really don't want to accept Christ. It's your choice. There's no sense in being wiped out because you're dumb. But you'll have to find some way to survive for seven years without buying food, selling food, or getting involved in modern society. The Indians survive down in the Mexican jungles. If the Indians can live off the land, you ought to be able to do it. There are still a few societies which are totally independent of the world system.

The Chocos Indians in the Darien providence of Panama are one such society. They're very industrious and grow their own food. They have their banana plantations and, when they come to market and sell, they always demand silver coins for their produce. When they return to the jungles they drill holes in the quarters and dimes and make necklaces. They have no use for the money, because they have everything they need. They are totally independent and self-sufficient. To the Chocos Indian money is not a means of exchange at all but a pretty decoration that shines in the sun. He simply wears it as jewelry.

These and others who are not dependent upon our society for their existence will not come under the economic pressure of the Antichrist. They will have a chance of surviving the great tribulation period, but not without suffering some of the worldwide plagues and judgments of God. No matter how you look at it it's a rough way to go.

When Jesus comes again, He will judge the nations. Those who have worshiped the beast, taken his mark, or worshiped his image will be at that point cast into the fire of Gehenna. The others who remain will be allowed to enter into the kingdom age.

REVELATION 20:5-6

But the rest of the dead lived not again until the thousand years were finished. This is the first resurrection. Blessed and holy is he that has part in the first resurrection: on such the second death has no power, but they shall be priests of God and of Christ, and shall reign with him a thousand years (Rev. 20:5–6).

To those on His right hand, Jesus will say, "Come, you blessed of My Father, inherit the kingdom prepared for you from the foundation of the world." To those on His left hand He'll say, "Depart from Me, you cursed, into Gehenna, prepared for Satan and his angels" (Matthew 25:34–41).

Gehenna wasn't prepared for man. It was prepared for Satan and his angels. But those people who choose to give allegiance to Satan and rebel with him against God will have their wish fulfilled throughout all eternity. They too will be cast into Gehenna.

Those who live into this age and survive the judgment of Christ when He returns will be allowed to live during the kingdom age when the earth is restored and begins to produce abundantly. The whole earth's surface and structure will be changed to the way it was when Adam and Eve were first upon the earth. There will be no rain upon the earth. Instead, moisture will condense at night and gently water the ground and plants. Everything will become fruitful and abundant. It will be Hawaii all over the earth!

When Adam sinned, God said, "Cursed is the ground for your sake... thorns also and thistles shall it bring forth to you... in the sweat of your face shall you eat bread" (Genesis 3:17–19). But that wasn't God's original intent. God had originally commanded the earth to produce abundantly to take care of man's needs. All you had to do was go out and pick food off the tree.

God will restore the earth, and longevity will be returned. You'll be able to live abundantly, unless you want to be wicked. Then you'll be cut off because the church will be here to enforce righteousness.

As the church, we will rule and reign with Christ. Our position will be the enforcers of righteousness. Jesus said to the church of Thyatira, "And he that overcomes, and keeps my works unto the end, to him will I give power over the nations: and he shall rule them with a rod of iron" (Rev. 2:26–27). There will be an ironclad rule of righteousness over the world. People who have survived the great tribulation and enter into the kingdom age will not be allowed to live in greed or sin. They will be ruled over with a rod of iron. "As the vessels of a potter shall they be broken to shivers" (Rev. 2:27). The thousand-year rule of Jesus Christ is going to be a fantastic time!

REVELATION 20:7-10

At the end of this thousand-year period, Satan will be released out of the *abyss*. Once again he is going to deceive the nations.

> And when the thousand years are expired, Satan shall be loosed out of his prison, and shall go out to deceive the

nations which are in the four quarters of the earth, Gog and Magog, to gather them together to battle: the number of whom is as the sand of the sea (Rev. 20:7–8).

The fact that amazes me is that so many people at this point will rebel against Jesus Christ.

The Last Rebels—Living under the ideal conditions of the kingdom age with the earth restored, people will be able to have very large and healthy families. There will be no sickness, disease, or suffering. People will live to be a thousand years old. At the end of the kingdom age the earth will probably be tremendously populated.

Many people wouldn't have had a chance to make a real choice for Jesus Christ, because they were forced to serve Christ during the Millennium. At the end of the thousand years, when Satan is released, they will have a choice to be either good or bad. Many will choose at that time to rebel against Jesus Christ. This is almost unthinkable, yet Satan will gather an army from the nations to try to destroy Christ.

Those of you who have gone up with Christ in the rapture and have returned with Him in your glorified bodies will not have any problem with Satan at this time There's no way Satan can tempt you. "Blessed and holy is he who takes part in the first resurrection: on such the second death has no power" (Rev. 20:6). There's no way you can be touched or affected by Satan's rebellion at this time. This last rebellion will be the testing time for those who have been forced to follow Jesus Christ during the thousand years. It will be their chance to decide whether or not they really want Christ.

This will reveal for all eternity the rebellious heart of man against the order and authority of God.

You may say, "Adam didn't know any better. He only had a few days in the Garden before he failed. How do you know that man would really fail if he had the chance? It's all because of the environment. We're trying to change man's environment so we can change man." No, the problem isn't the environment. It's that evil heart of man that rebels against God's authority.

Here are people who have enjoyed the benefits and the blessings of the kingdom age. They are living in the perfect environment of righteousness, peace, and love. When Satan is loosed, they will join his forces and actually invade the Holy Land. They will encircle the city of Jerusalem where Christ will be reigning on Mount Zion (Rev. 20:9). This invading army will be thoroughly and completely vanquished. Fire will come down from heaven to devour them.

> And they went up on the breadth of the earth, and compassed the camp of the saints about, and the beloved city: and fire came down from God out of heaven, and devoured them. And the devil that deceived them was cast into the lake of fire and brimstone, where the beast and the false prophet are, and shall be tormented day and night for ever and ever [literally "from the ages to the ages"] (Rev. 20:9–10).

This phrase, "from the ages to the ages," is the strongest Greek term possible to express eternity. There are those who teach that hell is not eternal. In a technical sense that is true. Hell (Hades) will give up the dead which are in it (Rev. 20:13). But there is a place of eternal punishment for those who have rebelled against God's order. It is called Gehenna, the lake of fire.

REVELATION 20:11-13

We now come to the great white throne judgment of God. This is the period of the second resurrection.

Daniel speaks of a resurrection from the dead: some unto everlasting life and some to eternal shame (Daniel 12:2). Actually, these two resurrections will be at least a thousand years apart.

The first resurrection will be that of the righteous dead who rise to live and reign with Christ during the Millennium. The rest of the dead will not live until the thousand years are expired

(Rev. 20:5). And then in Revelation 20 we have the second resurrection.

> I saw a great white throne, and Him that sat on it, from whose face the earth and the heaven fled away; and there was found no place for them. And I saw the dead, small and great [all the unrighteous who have lived up to this point], stand before God; and the books were opened: and another book was opened, which is the book of life: and the dead were judged out of those things which were written in the books, according to their works. And the sea gave up the dead which were in it; and death and hell delivered up the dead which were in them: and they were judged every man according to their works (Rev. 20:11–13).

Men in Space and Time—Verse 13 is interesting for it declares that the sea gives up the dead which are in it. It lists them in a separate category from those delivered up by death and hell. This gives rise to the theory that intelligent beings may have inhabited the earth before Adam, and were buried in a deluge by the seas.

When a person who is not a Christian dies now, he is in a waiting place called Hades, translated "hell" in your King James Bible. This place called Hades is actually in the center of the earth, and those unrighteous dead are in it. It doesn't matter if he's buried at sea or if he's cremated and his ashes are scattered from an airplane, his unsaved soul goes to hell. It would not stand to reason that, if the dead were buried at sea, the sea would give them up. No matter where he may be buried, if he's a sinner his soul is in hell. Yet, Revelation 20:13 tells us that death and hell gave up the dead which were in them separate from those dead that were given up by the sea.

We don't know if there were pre-Adamic creatures, and if there were, what they were like. We don't have any records and there's no way of knowing. They were destroyed, if they did indeed exist.

Genesis 1:1 is an account of original creation. Verse 2 may be translated, "But the earth became wasted and desolate and darkness was upon the face of the deep. And the Spirit of God moved upon the face of the waters." God may have destroyed the pre-Adamic race in the great cataclysmic upheaval when He allowed the waters to cover the face of the deep, thereby totally destroying their civilizations.

God placed Adam on the earth approximately six thousand years ago. The earth's age is at least several thousand years older. It doesn't seem reasonable that God would have created the earth and left it uninhabited for a great length of time.

It also doesn't seem likely that God would create anything without form and void. God has had such a beautiful design in all His creation. Isaiah said that God did not create the earth a waste but He created it to be inhabited (Isaiah 45:18).

By the same token, it doesn't seem logical that the earth is the only area where God would place created, intelligent beings. The Bible doesn't tell us anything about people on other planets, but would God create this entire vast universe and only choose one little part to populate? No reason exists for us to believe that we're exclusive in the universe.

Of course, God could have thrown the stars out into space just for your enjoyment. However, that doesn't seem likely to me. Having created the vast universe, He's probably populated other parts of it, too.

Yet, you are definitely unique. In all the universe, there's only one you. Man is unique in the universe. And God so loved this world, God so loved you, that He made provision for your salvation through Jesus Christ.

Choose Your Destiny—It's a mistake to think that death is the end. It's not the end. All the dead, small and great, stand before the great white throne judgment of God. The sea has given up the dead which are in it. Death and hell have spewed out their dead. The books are open and the dead are judged out of the things which are written in the books. It is a somewhat frightening thing that God keeps such records, but the deeds of your life have all been recorded. With God's ability, I imagine the records are quite complete. The dead will be judged according to their works (Rev. 20:12).

The Jews came to Jesus and said, "What shall we do, that we might work the works of God?" Jesus answered, "This is the work of God, that you believe on Him whom He has sent" (John 6:28–29). They'll be judged according to their works. They did not believe in Him. Jesus said,

> When He [the Holy Ghost] is come, He will reprove the world of sin, and of righteousness, and of judgment: of sin, because they believe not on Me (John 16:8–9).

Really, that's the only thing that will exclude a person from the heavenly kingdom—his failure to believe in God's provision for his sins through Jesus Christ. Jesus said,

> All manner of sin and blasphemy shall be forgiven unto men: but the blasphemy against the Holy Spirit shall not be forgiven unto men (Matthew 12:31).

The Holy Spirit is come to point out Jesus Christ as your Savior. If you reject the witness of the Holy Spirit, you're blaspheming and insulting the Spirit of grace. You're counting the blood of the covenant by which he was sanctified an unholy thing. Having rejected God's only path of salvation, there remains only that certain fearful looking forward to the fiery indignation of the wrath of God (Hebrews 10:27, 29).

Your sins were already judged on the cross. Jesus took God's wrath when He died on the cross in your place. You don't have to stand before God to face the consequences of your own sin.

If you stand at this great white throne judgment, you stand there because you have deliberately and willfully rejected God's plan of salvation through His Son, Jesus Christ. You have willfully and knowingly turned your back on God's way.

It doesn't take much imagination to picture the whole scene. You're standing in that multitude. Finally, your name is called as the recording angel reads down the book. You step out and stand there absolutely open and revealed. You step up, trembling before

God, the Creator of the universe. You say, "Just a minute, God. I can explain."

He says, "Take your time. You've got eternity."

"Now, Lord, let me tell You something. I really would have done it but there was this dude and he claimed to be a Christian. He was a big phony. He was going around ripping off everybody. He was such a big hypocrite that I decided, 'If that's what it's all about, I don't want anything to do with it!' "

God answers, "I didn't ask you to believe in any dude. I asked you to believe in My Son, Jesus Christ."

"Let me explain," you respond. "There were so many churches, and every one of them was claiming to be the right church. I was confused. I didn't know what church to go to in order to be a Christian."

God says, "I didn't tell you to go to any church to be a Christian. I told you to believe on My Son, to receive Him as your Lord and as your Savior."

One by one, every excuse you bring up will be wiped away until you'll be left without any defense. The books are open. You will be judged. The Bible says, "It is a fearful thing to fall into the hands of the living God" (Hebrews 10:31).

The Final Verdict—It isn't easy to get before this great white throne judgment of God. If you do make it that far, it's because you're really tough. First, you've trampled over Jesus Christ. You had to walk right over Him to get there. He's standing in your way to block you from facing judgment. He's standing in your path right now saying, "I love you. I gave Myself for you. I died in your place. I shed My blood so that your sins could be forgiven. I gave Myself for you to set you free from sin and to make you a new creature." You've got to trample right over Him.

Secondly, "They have counted the blood of the covenant by which he was sanctified an unholy thing." He shed His blood for your sin. The Bible says that "without shedding of blood is no remission [of sin]" (Hebrews 9:22).

The shedding of blood signified the giving of a life. In the Old Testament times the people of God had animal sacrifices. The shedding of blood signified that the penalty of sin was paid because a life was given (Leviticus 4; 17:11). God said in the beginning to Adam, "If you sin, you're surely going to die" (Genesis 2:17). That has been the wages of sin from the beginning and it has never been reduced. Today, the wages of sin is death (Romans 6:23).

Christ shed His blood for your salvation. If you refuse Him, you have to count the blood that He shed for you an unholy thing.

Thirdly, you have to insult the Spirit of grace because God's Holy Spirit is speaking to your heart now and saying, "That's the only way. Just give your life to Jesus Christ." The Spirit of God is saying, "You have sinned. Look, you are guilty. You need Jesus Christ. Go ahead and turn your life over to Him." But you have acted spitefully to the Spirit of grace. You are saying to the Holy Spirit, "Leave me alone! I'll do it my own way. I'll live my own life. Don't bother me!"

If you do those three things, I guarantee that one day I'll see you standing before the great white throne judgment of God. If you glance over at me, I'll say, "I told you. I'm sorry that you wouldn't believe."

God has done everything to save you. God isn't anxious to damn your soul. God said, "I have no pleasure in the death of the wicked... turn, turn from your evil ways; for why will you die?" (Ezekiel 33:11). God is love. In His love God has made provision for you. Reject God and His provisions and you have to suffer the consequence. God is bound by His Word to bring judgment against sin. That final day of judgment will come.

God is also very, very patient. Many people have erred because they've mistaken the patience of God for weakness. They think that God really won't punish sin. Don't deceive yourself. God is obligated to fulfill His Word, and He shall fulfill that which He said.

This scene we're reading in Revelation is not something out of somebody's imagination. God spoke to John through the angel and declared these things that are going to happen. John wrote them down so that you might be warned.

REVELATION 20:14-15

> And death and hell were cast into the lake of fire [Gehenna]. This is the second death. And whosoever was not found written in the book of life was cast into Gehenna (Rev. 20:14–15).

The Book of Life—God keeps the books, and there's one book which God keeps that you should make certain your name is in—the Book of Life. Whosoever's name was not found written in the Book of Life was cast into Gehenna.

There's one way you can be assured that your name is written in the Book of Life. That is by asking Jesus Christ to come into your life and wash you from your sin. For "as many as received him, to them gave he power to become the sons of God, even to them that believe on his name" (John 1:12).

I can read about the great white throne judgment of God and have no fears and no qualms. It doesn't shake me because my sins have already been judged. My name is in the Book of Life.

The only judgment seat I'll stand before will be the judgment seat of Christ (2 Corinthians 5:10), which is an entirely different thing. This judgment seat is like the judge's seat in the Olympic races. I've run in a race and won. I come up to the judge's seat, and the judge places the crown of life upon my head. Paul said, "Do you not know that they who run in a race run all, but one receives the prize? So run, that you might obtain" (1 Corinthians 9:24).

You're going to be at one of two judgment seats. You'll either appear before the judgment seat of Christ, or you'll appear before the great white throne judgment of God. Which judgment seat you appear before is absolutely up to you, for your choice determines your destiny.

The great white throne judgment is a very tragic scene. In fact, it is the most tragic event in the history of the world. A person who stands before the great white throne judgment of God hears only one sentence pronounced: Lost.

However, this isn't the end of the Revelation. Revelation 21 opens up a new and glorious phase—the eternal phase where God creates a new heaven and new earth. Sin is not even involved. We dwell now with God forever.

Emergency—I read of a farmer who was walking home one day along the railroad tracks. Evening was approaching and he lit his lantern. As he was walking along, he came to a section of the track where the rail was split and broken. He looked at his watch and realized that a train with several hundred passengers heading towards Chicago would be passing by in a few minutes. He knew that, if the train hit the broken section of track, many people would lose their lives.

He started running down the tracks in the direction from which the train was coming. After a while he heard the whistle of the train in the distance. He increased his speed, even though he was almost totally exhausted.

Finally, he saw the light of the train as it approached. He went running right down the middle of the tracks towards that onrushing train waving his lantern. At the last moment he jumped aside and threw his lantern up through the cab of the locomotive and hit the engineer right in the face. The engineer pulled on the emergency brake and the wheels began to throw fire. The train was brought to a halt a few feet short of the broken rail.

Some of you are headed down the track towards destruction, and God's hitting you square in the face with the Gospel of Jesus Christ. He wants to stop you in your mad dash to hell. You can do one of two things. You can say that the man is a lunatic. He's making it up. And you can keep on going towards your absolute destruction.

Or you can put on the brakes and receive Jesus Christ. And you can be sure that it will never happen to you, for God will save you from the wrath to come.

CHAPTER 21
OUR NEW ADDRESS

REVELATION 21:1

We have now passed beyond the realm of time into eternity. The last marking of time was the thousand-year reign of Christ upon the earth. After the millennial reign of Christ, we enter into timelessness. Everything is now forever.

John says, "And I saw a new heaven and a new earth" (Rev. 21:1).

Peter tells us that our present heaven and earth will be destroyed one day. The earth and all the universe will melt with a fervent heat. Things will be dissolved, going up in a gigantic explosion. He said that we "look for new heavens and a new earth in which righteousness dwells" (2 Peter 3:10–13).

In Isaiah God said, "Behold, I create new heavens and a new earth: and the former shall not be remembered, nor come into mind" (Isaiah 65:17). It is interesting that the word *create* in Isaiah is the Hebrew word *"bara,"* which is also used in Genesis 1:1. "In the beginning God created [bara] the heaven and the earth." *Bara* in Hebrew means "to make something out of nothing," which only God can do. God uses the same Hebrew word *bara* when He speaks of creating the new heavens and the new earth; not a "reforming" (*asah*) of the existing orders, but the total new creation of something out of nothing.

In Revelation 21 we read, "I saw a new heaven and a new earth: for the first heaven and the first earth were passed away; and there was no more sea" (Rev. 21:1).

Three-fourths of the earth's surface is now covered by water, the oceans and the seas. There will be no sea on the earth which God creates in the new kingdom. The purpose of the sea and its salts is to collect and neutralize the pollutants so that the earth is habitable for man. Where there are no pollutants, as in the new earth, seas are not necessary. And if you happen to love sailing, God will have something much better for you!

REVELATION 21:2-7

> And I John saw the holy city, new Jerusalem, coming down from God out of heaven, prepared as a bride adorned for her husband. And I heard a great voice out of heaven saying, Behold, the tabernacle of God is with men, and he will dwell with them, and they shall be his people, and God himself shall be with them, and be their God. And God shall wipe away all tears from their eyes; and there shall be no more death, neither sorrow, nor crying, neither shall there be any more pain: for the former things are passed away (Rev. 21:24).

The New Jerusalem—All the glorious bliss of that eternal kingdom! Rebellion will be put out once and for all from God's universe. God will again reign as sovereign Lord. One God, one authority, one rule, one government of light and life will again rule the entire universe. What a glorious universe that shall be! No tears, no crying, no death, no sorrow, no pain.

> And he that sat upon the throne said, Behold. I make all things new. And he said unto me, Write: for these words are true and faithful. And he said unto me, It is done. I am Alpha and Omega, the beginning and the end. I will give unto him who is thirsty of the fountain of the water of life freely. He that overcomes shall inherit all things; and I will be his God, and he shall be my son (Rev. 21:5–7).

"Come, you blessed of my Father," Jesus will say, "inherit the kingdom prepared for you from the foundation of the world" (Matthew 25:34). "Inherit all things," He's going to say. "It's all yours! Just enjoy it." You'll have a new body in which you can probably roam the universe and explore the vastness of God's glorious creation. Note again the declaration, "These words are faithful and true."

REVELATION 21:8-10

> But the fearful, and unbelieving, and the abominable, and murderers, and whoremongers, and sorcerers, and idolaters, and all liars, shall have their part in the lake which burns with fire and brimstone: which is the second death (Rev. 21:8).

What a sharp contrast to the New Jerusalem. Yet, God lays it out for all to see. You can have your choice. Choose your destiny. Isn't it ridiculous to choose to rebel against God? Many say, "I don't know if it's true or not!" In reality, you choose to believe or not to believe. What do you have to lose? Dare you gamble when the stakes are so high?

> And there came unto me one of the seven angels which had the seven vials full of the seven last plagues, and talked with me, saying, Come, I will show you the bride, the Lamb's wife. And he carried me away in the spirit to a great and high mountain, and showed me that great city, the holy Jerusalem, descending out of heaven from God (Rev. 21:9–10).

One day you'll take up your residence in this city. It's the city where the church is to dwell.

REVELATION 21:11-12

The angel showed John that great city "having the glory of God: and her light was like unto a stone most precious, even like a jasper stone, clear as crystal [like a diamond]; And had a wall great and high, and had twelve gates, and at the gates twelve angels, and names written thereon, which are the names of the twelve tribes of the children of Israel" (Rev. 21:12). The number twelve is a very prominent number throughout the New Jerusalem.

This city will be inhabited by both the twelve tribes of Israel (those who, by faith, were looking forward to Jesus Christ) and the church. The book of Hebrews talks about those men of faith in the Old Testament—Abraham, Enoch, Noah, and others—who "died in faith, not having received the promises, but having seen them afar off... [they] embraced them, and confessed that they were strangers and pilgrims on the earth... [they were looking] for a city which has foundations, whose builder and maker is God" (Hebrews 11:13, 10).

Enoch, Noah, Abraham, Jacob, and Isaiah were actually looking for this city that the angel is showing now to John. The city which has foundations whose maker and builder is God: the Holy City, the New Jerusalem, the City of God coming down from heaven. God spoke to Abraham and these other men about this city. They died in faith not having received the promise but looked forward to it.

We, too, are strangers and pilgrims on this earth. We know that we won't be here forever. We're looking for a city which has foundations whose maker and builder is God. This city has a great wall with twelve gates. The names of the twelve tribes are written on these twelve entrances. At each one there stands an angel. He will probably welcome you as you enter into the gate of the city—"Praise God! Welcome!"

REVELATION 21:13-21

On the east side of the city there are "three gates; on the north three gates; on the south three gates; and on the west three gates. And the wall of the city had twelve foundations [great foundation stones in the wall of the city], and in them the names of the twelve apostles of the Lamb" (Rev. 21:13–14).

This angel that talked with John "had a golden reed to measure the city, and the gates thereof, and the wall thereof. And the city lies foursquare [as a cube], and the length is as large as the breadth: and he measured the city with the reed, [and it was] twelve thousand furlongs [approximately fifteen hundred miles]. The length and the breadth and the height of it are equal"

(Rev. 21:15–16). There are over three billion cubic miles in this city. Some city, to say the least!

The New Jerusalem is approximately the size of the moon. The moon, of course, is a sphere, but this creation is a cube. As far as we know, there aren't any cubed astronomical bodies.

I don't know why God has shaped all the bodies that we can observe in a sphere, but I'm certain that He had a purpose. Yet, here is a cubed city coming down from heaven. It will orbit the earth like the moon, perhaps a bit closer.

How are we going to dwell in this city? I don't know. It may be like a huge skyscraper. If it is, you could have fifteen hundred mile-high stories. If you gave everybody a cubic mile to live in, the heavens could hold over 3.3 billion people. If you allowed for a greater density of population, you could fit in a lot more people.

A woman once said, "I don't know if there'll be enough room in heaven." If not, take a star! There are enough stars so that everyone could have his own galaxy of stars. There are billions of galaxies and, within each one, billions of stars. We'll inherit all these things! There'll be plenty of room for everybody.

Perhaps Jesus was referring to this city when He said, "In my Father's house are many mansions... I go to prepare a place for you" (John 14:2). This is the city whose architect and builder is God. This is the city that Christ has gone to prepare for you. When you get there He will say, "Glad to see you here! Let me show you the place that is set for you."

It is exciting to contemplate what this city will be like. The earth in which we now live is a beautiful place. Some spots in Hawaii that man hasn't yet corrupted are extremely gorgeous. There are some places in California that are really breathtaking. As you look at the earth and its beauty, just realize that God took it from being without form and void, refurbished it, and put man on it—all in about six days. If He can make our earth this beautiful in six days, imagine what your place will be like. He's been working on it for almost two thousand years!

Heavenly Specifications—John measured the wall. It was "a hundred and forty four cubits [about two hundred feet high], according to the measure of a man, that is, of the angel" (Rev. 21:17). A cubit is the distance from your elbow to your fingertip. A span is the distance between your thumb and your baby finger. This is the way they measured everything in biblical times.

"And the building of the wall of it was of jasper [clear stone like a diamond]: and the city was pure gold, like unto clear glass" (Rev. 21:18). In other words, the gold was so pure that it was transparent. We are unable to refine gold to such a pure state.

> And the foundations of the wall of the city were garnished with all manner of precious stones. The first foundation was jasper; the second, sapphire; the third, a chalcedony; the fourth, an emerald; the fifth, sardonyx; the sixth, sardius; the seventh, chrysolyte; the eighth, beryl; the ninth, a topaz; the tenth, a chrysoprasus; the eleventh, a jacinth; the twelfth, an amethyst (Rev. 21:19–20).

These are the stones that were in the breastplate of the priest in the Old Testament (Exodus 28:17–20). Imagine these beautiful, precious gems in the foundation of the wall, with the wall itself being of jasper!

> And the twelve gates were twelve pearls; every several gate was of one pearl." One huge pearl making up the gate! "And the street of the city was pure gold, as it were transparent glass (Rev. 21:21).

When you read this, you realize how foolish it is for someone to say that God needs your money. If He can make a city like this, your phony American currency would mean nothing to Him. Your fifty-cents piece isn't even real silver anymore. God can create whatever He wants. God is not poor. God is not lacking. God doesn't need your money.

However, He does give to us the privilege of investing our money in His eternal kingdom and the things that count for His eternal kingdom. That is a privilege, not an obligation. It isn't a duty. He didn't have to allow us that privilege. But He did. It's one of the greatest privileges that I have. God says, "If you give to Me, I'll give you dividends like you can't believe!" (Malachi 3:10).

REVELATION 21:22-27

John looked around for the temple and said, "I saw no temple therein: for the Lord God Almighty and the Lamb are the temple of it" (Rev. 21:22). You don't need any temple where God and Christ dwell. "And the city had no need of the sun, neither of the moon, to shine in it: for the glory of God did lighten it, and the Lamb is the light thereof" (Rev. 21:23).

Imagine the glowing glory of God as all these beautiful stones reflect the beauty of God. The transparent, golden streets are aglow throughout the entire city. Our minds can't even conceive of such brilliance and luminosity.

God has His own lighting system. No sun, no moon—just an iridescent glow from His glory throughout the whole city. There'll be no energy crisis in this city.

Looking up from the earth and seeing this Holy City in its orbit will be an extremely beautiful sight.

And the nations of them which are saved shall walk in the light of it. [It seems that the New Jerusalem gives light to the earth]. And the kings of the earth do bring their glory and honor into it. And the gates of it shall not be shut at all by day: for there shall be no night there (Rev. 21:24–25).

In the ancient cities there were many walls with gates. The walls were for protection, and the gates were shut at night. You won't need protection in this city, however. God and Christ are dwelling there. There is no night, so there is no shutting of the gates. They're always open.

And they [the kings of the earth] shall bring the glory and honor of the nations into it. And there shall in no wise enter into it any thing that defiles, neither whatsoever works abomination, or makes a lie: but they which are written in the Lamb's book of life (Rev. 21:26–27).

We who are privileged to be chosen by God to believe in Jesus Christ and to be conformed to His image will have the right to enter in and inhabit this glorious city. What a blessing!

CHAPTER 22
PEACE LIKE A RIVER

REVELATION 22:1-2

A nd he showed me a pure river of water of life, clear as crystal, proceeding out of the throne of God and of the Lamb. In the midst of the street of it, and on either side of the river, there was the tree of life, which bare twelve manner of fruits, and yielded her fruit every month: and the leaves of the tree were for the healing of the nations (Rev. 22:1–2).

John describes a river of life in this new city; however, it's not like any river around here!

When we return with Jesus Christ to spend a thousand years on this earth in His kingdom reign, Jesus will set His foot on the Mount of Olives, splitting it in the middle. This will cause a great valley to form. A river will come out of the new temple in the earthly city of Jerusalem. This river will be divided. One portion will flow to the Dead Sea and the other portion will flow down to the Mediterranean Sea (Zechariah 14:4, 8). When the river comes down to the Dead Sea the waters of the Dead Sea will be healed, and there will be a multitude of many varieties of fish (Ezekiel 47:1–12).

The river that flows from the temple in the earthly Jerusalem is not the same river of life that proceeds out of the new heaven and new earth. However, there are definite similarities between the two rivers.

On the banks on either side of the earthly river there are trees which bear a different fruit every month. Ezekiel describes them as similar to the trees by the river of life in the New Jerusalem.

As I have mentioned before, God has designed earthly things to be similar to heavenly things, especially around Jerusalem. There are always those who claim that the river of life is figurative and not literal. But there is a danger in saying this. If God calls it a river but it's really not a river, and God says it's a tree but it's really not a tree, then how are we to believe what God says? If God didn't mean what He said, then why didn't God say what He meant?

When someone says that God didn't mean what He said, and then goes into a fancy explanation to spiritualize the text, he completely destroys the meaning. I take it to be a river of life with crystal pure water in the New Jerusalem. And I plan to take a drink from it when I get there.

REVELATION 22:3-6A

And there shall be no more curse (Rev. 22:3).

At the present time, the earth is under a curse. God said to Adam, "Cursed is the ground for your sake... thorns also and thistles shall it bring forth to you" (Genesis 3:17–18). Man is also under a curse. God said, "In the sweat of your face you shall eat bread, till you return unto the ground; for out of it you were taken: for dust you are, and unto dust shall you return" (Genesis 3:19). Earning your bread by the sweat of your brow is also a part of the curse. It's the result of man's sin.

In the new earth there will be no more curse. This doesn't mean that we'll be sitting around and twiddling our thumbs. It means that we'll have a whole new way of life.

But the throne of God and of the Lamb shall be in it; and his servants shall serve him: And they shall see his face; and his name shall be in their foreheads (Rev. 22:34).

I've tried to imagine the emotion that a person will experience when he looks into the face of Jesus Christ. It will be glorious!

And there shall be no night there; and they need no candle, neither light of the sun; for the Lord God gives them light and they shall reign for ever and ever. And he

said unto me, These sayings are faithful and true
(Rev. 22:5–6a).

Jesus is saying, "I know it sounds far out. I know it sounds
wild. I know it's hard to grasp and conceive. It sounds like a fairy
tale. But these things are faithful and true." There is nothing more
sure than the prophecies of God's Word. We have "a more sure
word of prophecy" (2 Peter 1:19).

REVELATION 22:6B-21

And the Lord God of the holy prophets sent his angel to
show unto his servants the things which must shortly be
done. Behold, I come quickly: blessed is he that keeps the
sayings of the prophecy of this book (Rev. 22:6b–7).

This is a repeat of the promised blessing in chapter 1:3 for
those who keep the sayings of this book.

You ask, "What does Jesus mean 'I come quickly'? John wrote
that almost two thousand years ago, didn't he?" Yes. And the Bible
says, "One day is with the Lord as a thousand years, and a
thousand years as one day" (2 Peter 3:8). So, it's been a couple of
days—almost!

"I, John, saw these things, and heard them. And when I had
heard and seen, I fell down to worship before the feet of the angel
which showed me these things" (Rev. 22:8). This is the second
time that John makes the mistake of worshiping the angel.

Then said he unto me, See that you do it not: for I am
your fellow servant, and of your brethren the prophets,
and of them which keep the sayings of this book: worship
God. And he said unto me, Seal not the sayings of the
prophecy of this book: for the time is at hand. He that is
unjust, let him be unjust still: and he which is filthy, let
him be filthy still: and he that is righteous, let him be
righteous still: and he that is holy, let him be holy still.
And, behold [now Jesus is speaking to John], I come
quickly; and My reward is with Me, to give every man
according as his work shall be (Rev. 22:9–12).

08

WHAT THE WORLD IS COMING TO

Jesus continues,

> I am Alpha and Omega, the beginning and the end, the first and the last. Blessed are they that do his commandments, that they may have right to the tree of life, and may enter in through the gates into the city. For without are dogs, and sorcerers, and whoremongers, and murderers, and idolaters, and whosoever loves and makes a lie. I Jesus have sent My angel to testify unto you these things in the churches. I am the Root and the Offspring of David, and the Bright and Morning Star. And the Spirit and the bride say, Come. And let him that hears say, Come. And let him that is thirsty come. And whosoever will, let him take the water of life freely.
>
> For I testify unto every man that hears the words of the prophecy of this book, If any man shall add unto these things, God shall add unto him the plagues that are written in this book: and if any man shall take away from the words of the book of this prophecy, God shall take away his part out of the book of life, and out of the holy city, and from the things which are written in this book (Rev. 22:13–19).

After that kind of warning, any man would be a fool to tamper with the book of Revelation. Yet men do.

> He which testifies these things says, Surely I come quickly. Amen. Even so, come, Lord Jesus. The grace of our Lord Jesus Christ be with you all. Amen (Rev. 22:20–21).

The Beginning and The End—There is a very sharp contrast between the first three chapters of Genesis and the last two chapters of Revelation. Let me list some of these contrasts for you.

In Genesis we read of the beginning of this world. In Revelation we have the end of it. "In the beginning God created the heaven and the earth (Gen. 1:1); "And I saw a new heaven and a new earth" (Rev. 21:1).

"God called the dry land Earth; and the gathering together of the waters called he Seas" (Gen. 1:10); "And there was no more sea" (Rev. 21:1).

"The darkness he called Night" (Gen. 1:5); "There shall be no night there" (Rev. 21:25).

"God made two great lights; the greater light to rule the day, and the lesser light to rule the night" (Gen. 1:16); "The city had no need of the sun, neither of the moon" (Rev. 21:23).

"In the day that you eat thereof [of the tree of knowledge of good and evil] you shall surely die" (Gen. 2:17); "There shall be no more death" (Rev. 21:4).

"I will greatly multiply your sorrow and your conception [pain]" (Gen. 3:16); "Neither shall there be any more pain" (Rev. 21:4).

"Cursed is the ground for your sake" (Gen. 3:17); "There shall be no more curse" (Rev. 22:3).

Satan appears as a deceiver (Gen. 3:1); Satan disappears forever (Rev. 20:10). Man is driven from the tree of life (Gen. 3:22–24); the tree of life is available for all (Rev. 22:2). Man is driven from God's presence (Gen. 3:24); "And they shall see His face" (Rev. 22:4). Man's first home was by a river (Gen. 2:10); man's eternal home is by God's river (Rev. 22:1).

The final chapter of a book is always exciting because it ties everything together. All the mysteries, the intrigue, and the questions are brought together. The answers come to us as God unfolds the beauties of His love and reveals the eternal kingdom that He has planned for those who love Him and serve Him. What a glorious and blessed time we are looking forward to!

Realizing all these things as Jesus said, "Surely I come quickly," John naturally responded, "Amen. Even so, come, Lord Jesus."

Let's get on with that Eternal Kingdom!

STUDY NOTES

STUDY NOTES

STUDY NOTES

PROPHECY RESOURCES
BY CHUCK SMITH

THE RAPTURE: ARE YOU READY?

One day millions of people, young and old, are going to be snatched up into the air to join Jesus Christ in heaven. Who is going? What will happen on earth after the rapture? Join Pastor Chuck Smith as he expounds upon the Scriptures detailing the raputre of the church and the great tribulation. See for yourself what the Bible says about the rapture and what every Christian should be doing in anticipation for this great day!

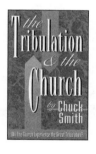

THE TRIBULATION & THE CHURCH

Will the church of Christ experience the great tribulation? Pastor Chuck gives biblical reasons why he believes that the church will not be here during the tribulation. This book expounds upon the rapture, the first resurrection, the 70 weeks prophecy of Daniel and the Book of Revelation.

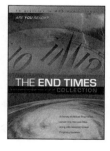

THE END TIMES COLLECTION

A survey of biblical prophecies concerning the Last Days including Pastor Chuck's Prophecy Updates. Chuck Smith examines current events as pieces in the End Times puzzle. The pieces are coming together and are considered in view of the Scriptures. Includes Bible studies from Daniel, Ezekiel, Zechariah, Matthew, and other related commentaries.

THE BOOK OF REVELATION AUDIO COMMENTARY

Known for his ability to make the Scriptures come alive, Pastor Chuck Smith explains and dissects Revelation—the only book of the Bible that declares a blessing on those who read, hear, and keep it! Taken from a recent series on the Book of Revelation, these messages will help you understand one of the most enigmatic and prophetic books of the Bible.

THE FINAL CURTAIN

Chuck Smith provides insight into God's prophetic plan and shows how current events are leading to the time when one climactic battle will usher in eternity. This pocket-sized book deals with such subjects as Bible prophecy, the Middle East, the world, and the role of the Antichrist. *The Final Curtain*, is a compact hard-hitting exposé on the last days of human history.

THE SIGNS OF HIS COMING AUDIO COMMENTARY

Wars, rumors of wars, famines, diseases, earthquakes, false prophets, the mark of the beast...What does the Bible tell us about the last days? Can we know when Jesus will return? Pastor Chuck Smith explains prophecy in light of today's changing world. Some messages include The Seventy Weeks of Daniel, Signs of His Coming, Expecting His Return, and a prophecy update.

TIME IS SHORT AUDIO COMMENTARY

Considering the ever present possibility of terrorist attacks and war in the Middle East, *Time is Short* is a collection of messages of hope and vision, studies on sanctification and prophecy that will inspire and encourage you to get involved in the Lord's work in these last days. Guest speakers include Chuck Smith, Brian Brodersen, Don McClure, and Jon Courson.

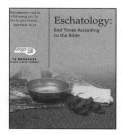

ESCHATOLOGY AUDIO COMMENTARY

Join various senior pastors of Calvary Chapel as they discuss the end times according to the Bible. Studies include: A complete commentary overview of the book of Daniel; Evolution and the New Age Movements; Expecting His Return; Heresies that have crept into the church; the rapture of the church; and the signs of the times.

For information about additional products
or to be added to our e-mail list
for product updates,
please contact:

THE WORD
FOR TODAY

P.O. Box 8000, Costa Mesa, CA 92628
800-272-WORD (9673)
www.twft.com • E-mail: info@twft.com